Live Your CORE

Attaining Absolute Happiness through Mandala Mindfulness

Dr. SHIPRA BHATIA

ISBN 979-8-89066-950-6

CONTENTS

PROLOGUE

Hello! This book is my enriched experience with the most satisfying Art I have ever encountered. An Art that sees through you and brings out the most beautiful and meaningful Art learnings of life resting deep within the ocean of our thoughts, emotions, and experiences.

Let's once again travel, but now together, to explore Mandala Art with me. Mandalas, which are circular patterns, existed in our life much earlier than humans of varied cultures, religions, and philosophies discovered them. Nature, our soul crafter, has forms of Mandala in every sphere. Mandala plays its poignant melody in celestial bodies, down on Land, or across the oceans.

The urge to have a circular harmony within our five feet body is inevitable. That's why so many people across the globe are getting fascinated by this miraculous Art without even knowing the fundamental change or transformation they are undergoing, even just by looking at Mandalas around. The Symmetry of a sunflower, snowflake, ripples in the water, the milky way in the galaxy, and a deluge of other natural mandala forms create a pleasant feeling and evoke calmness and peace within.

We, humans, seek wholeness and completeness in our environment. Mandalas, by nature, work as a catalyst to curb this craving and find holistic growth and self-development by introspecting our innate emotions and thoughts that shape our perceptions and lead to positive and negative reactions.

Professor Carl Jung, the Father of Mandalas, has said, "Until you make the unconscious conscious, it will direct your life, and you will call it fate." Mandalas connect our subconscious mind with our conscious being.

Both reflective and creative, Mandalas help unravel layers that we consciously stack one after the other, trying to avoid any unpleasant confrontation with our hidden emotional state. Once we get into the comfort zone of acceptance of our reflections, we automatically enter the creative area.

Mandala making, when done intuitively without holding ourselves or putting restrictions or constraints on our thoughts, brings the best positive outcomes to make us a better version of ourselves. Mandala's creation is primarily living in the moment. A reflective composition helps to delve deeper into the Self and bring out stories or snippets of life that profoundly impact our psyche.

We embrace positive and negative life memories that reflect prominently in our daily behavior and conduct. Sometimes conspicuously and often inconspicuously, our dormant life state and drives turn into our present directions. We tend to stray from our path because it's not us steering life's wheel but the static voices that control our minds and forbid us to listen to our hearts. In such jittery situations, we need to surrender. Surrender entirely to a zone where we are safe, and we get time to reflect impartially on our past actions, the anticipated and unanticipated reactions, and the desired course of action we need to follow to steer the wheel by having complete control of our minds. "Let not the mind master you, but you be the master of your mind."- Daisaku Ikeda. The Mandala is a safe space where all such hidden stories reflect without being judgmental. We get to navigate our path. Confront ourselves, appreciate the positive traits, and work on areas that need our attention and focus to polish and refine ourselves.

Creative Mandalas are mostly an inner urge to break boundaries and satisfy our hunger for acknowledgment, appreciation, and learning. Mandalas may originate from a creative space and lead to a reflective precinct or deliberately begin from an inner reflection and connect to our creative transformation. Mandala help in our self-development, growth, and happiness. We need to trust the process. Even coloring a Mandala or gazing at one can generate positive vibes and self-awakening. One need not be a seasoned artist to create his Universe. Mandala-making is a process of healing oneself from negative regressive emotions. Finding 'Self' in the process is quintessential, and focusing on perfection is secondary. With consistent practice, understanding, and perseverance, even the creative Self gets polished. Mandalas emerge from a single dot. Just a center is all we need to create a wholesome self.

There is no one way to create a Mandala. There are no rules or regulations to abide by, just a circular boundary. Either we start from our core, the central point, and move outwards, absorbing our inner emotions, or we may also start from the outer circle and move inverted, designing our unique path to find our core.

This book will be helpful for all those creative enthusiasts who have been long fascinated with the art form and want to have a hands-on experience with it, for those who have no artistic skills but still, their passion for making authentic Art is alive. Waiting for that little encouragement or push to dive and swim through their blues.

Mandala-making can serve as a reliable pathfinder for people who have lost their path or are searching for their calling and seeking to find themselves. You have outplayed yourself if you are overwhelmed with your situations or emotions. If maintaining your sanity gets complicated in the daily trials of life, then it's high time for introspection. It's a time when self-love and self-acceptance need priority. Mandala can aid in the process and be a healing tool.

Mandalas can be an experimental art therapy for special needs, catering to all age groups. It can stir and strengthen cognitive development, increase attention span, and refine motor skills.

It's a process to enjoy. A solid emotion to live. Experience completeness and wholesomeness. This urge can only be satisfied once we put it into action, no matter what it's form or intent turn out to be. Grab your paper, pen, compass, color, paint, to make a fresh start. The fact that this book is in your hands right now marks the initiation of the 'change.' The process has already begun. Now don't hold back. Find yourself NOW!

MANDALA – MY CALLING

I am not an artist by profession. Arts, however, has been my calling since childhood. Colors, in general, attracted me. Black and Red fascinated me the most. I never considered painting and Art an option for career growth because I came from a time and place where Art was just a hobby and never taken as an option worth exploring. I took my brother to be my idol and followed his footsteps. I studied hard, excelled in my chosen field, and was awarded a Doctorate of Philosophy in Management. I pursued my career as a Professor teaching my favorite subjects and building an eternal bond with my students that have lasted very special to me to date. But somewhere in the hustle and bustle of life, the priorities changed. The need for the moment demanded a complete detour from the self-chosen path. The best thing that ever happened to me was a connection with my mentor Dr. Daisaku Ikeda whom I have never met personally but have known through his teachings, writings and struggles for World Peace. His actions in realizing his dreams are exemplary, and for me, my mentor became my friend, philosopher, and guide who took me through every single storm of life and encouraged me to face it undauntingly without begrudging my life.

I overcame many challenges. Becoming a parent to a special needs, differently able child was my most precious blessing. My life transformed when I understood the meaning of absolute happiness. My children are my world, and my family my raison d'etre. Amidst these happy emotions, there was a void. A vacant fragment within me that constantly nudged me to find my true calling. I took Art as a means to fill that little void, only to find my awakening and 'Live my Core' through my spiritual Self. Always hooked to Mandala Art, I took it as a fish takes to water. I needed more formal knowledge about the subject to plunge into it. I started with a small piece of paper and a pen, initially doing it as a creative reflection. I loved to form patterns, coloring them for hours and hours and feeling more energized instead of fatigued. In no time, Mandala became a part of my life. The more I practiced it, the more intrigued I became with the subject and the form, and I started researching its existence. I was stunned to know the expanse of this beholding Art. From a creative reflection, I slowly moved to a reflective creative. I could see my life in the Art I created intuitively. I could see all these emotions in my mandalas; Stressful relationships, stillbirth, agony, financial issues, loss of loved ones, trapped emotions, pain, etc. But I was looking for happiness free from all constraints, independent, and not confined to the absence of the above negative emotions. True happiness lies in the struggles of life. One can be joyful even in pain. I found my life's mission in my Mandala Art.

I always preferred to avoid copying people's Art or patterns. There was an inner voice to be true to my feelings and create a unique, original piece of Art that reflected my being. From an amateur artist to a lifelong seeker, every Art I created had something of ME. My Art unknowingly resonated with symbols that have a significant meaning in the Mandala art carried out for ages in various cultures like Hinduism, Buddhism, and many more. Initially, I couldn't make meaning out of the lines, patterns, and color choices I made instinctively. Still, slowly and gradually, as I proceeded further, I found that I could release my negative emotions through my Art. Patterns started making much sense to me. I could see my current moment's reflection in my Art. When I felt disdained, in utter despair, I made patterns haphazardly, struggling to connect with the thought and the creation I put on the paper or the surface I chose to work upon. Still, on days when I was delighted and excited, my Art surprised me. My color choices were striking.

My patterns had a connection, a meaning. Moreover, when my mind was in utter chaos, I could interpret it in my creation. Thoroughly researching on literature available and getting into the psyche of eminent names associated with Mandala, like Carl Jung and Fischer, helped me connect to the subject's depth. I was amazed to find the amount of massive literature available on the internet and in libraries. Mandala and healing go hand-in-hand. Mandala helped me stay calm and in a controlled phase at larger intervals, enabling me to further pass it on to my differently able son.

Dealing with hyperactivity and meltdown isn't easy, but the Art therapy certainly eased the flow of negativity and control situations that otherwise could have been quite overwhelming.

Sometimes I could dream of patterns and concepts I wanted to intertwine with other art forms. Some came out brilliant, while few were complicated to understand. My inner voice got a medium of expression. We often keep things to ourselves until they stack up and release in an unpleasant episode, but art aids in liberating oneself from these trapped senses. I experimented with Mandala with fluid Art, Indian folk arts, coffee art, texture art, wood engravings, etc., to name a few. Each of the pieces was enticing and satisfying.

Analyzing Mandalas is a tedious process, especially for someone else. The earnestness and authenticity of the natural emotion in a particular moment can be validated only by the person undergoing those sentiments. I learned to journal my thoughts while making a Mandala. Before I initiated my Art, I ensured to pen down the real honest feelings I underwent in that time frame. As the process flowed further, the transformation or realization, vengeance or gratitude, reminiscence or repression, I could visualize clearly and write my emotions in my journal stemmed into a positive healing process. The book includes the need and process of journaling while creating a healing Mandala.

This book culminates all my learnings in creating, recreating, correcting, and healing myself, my Universe. The book also highlights the crux of the immense literature on the subject. The significance of Symmetrical and asymmetrical aspects is also taken care of. The presence of the Mandala and its various kinds, prevalent in different cultures and religions since centuries ago, gives the Art form its roots of origin and is widespread across the globe. Mandala, whether made from a reflective, creative aspect or a creative, reflective process, is a personal choice and inner calling. There is no right or wrong process. It's just a conscious choice leading to the ultimate core. Mandala and the Ten Worlds, an insight that draws reality from our daily life, is one unique relatable feature incorporated in this book. I have personally analyzed a few of my creative and reflective artwork here to impart a better understanding of the Self and the moment in which that the Self-originated. The anatomy of colors, patterns, and symbols gives a broader vision to the creations. My spiritual awakening owes a lot to this Art. This little effort in compiling my experiences with the graphical representation of my Universe will also guide you to travel your journey and create beautiful memories ahead.

Chapter – 02

EVOLUTION OF MANDALA

Origin of Mandala

Mandalas originated around 560 BC. Shakyamuni Buddha, whom we also revere as Gautam Buddha, left his royal palace and luxurious life in search of truth and answers to relieve humanity from the sufferings of birth, aging, sickness, and death. Gautam Buddha finally attained enlightenment through intense meditation. He revealed the eight noble paths through which any ordinary soul could achieve enlightenment. He preached the strategy of the Lotus Sutra propounded by Nichiren Daishonin, who was born in Japan. The teachings are widespread across various parts of India. Staunch followers and monks started revering Buddha and established their first community of monks called 'Sangha.' These Buddhist monks traveled across multiple regions worldwide through the Silk Road, the trade route connecting the East and the West.

The primary source of disseminating the knowledge gained and keeping track of routes in imprinted cardinal directions, painted Mandalas, was carried from place to place. Tibet, China, and Japan were the places where such Mandalas flourished to practice various tasks and purposes. Eventually, they became an eminent part of Hinduism and other religious practices.

Mandala the inner voice of your core that wants to be heard loud and clear. A perfect melody that resonates well with your heart, mind, and soul together, revealing your innate desires, perceptions, emotions, thoughts, and aspirations.

The literal meaning of Mandala in Sanskrit (The classical language of the Indo-Aryan) refers to a 'circle.' Life is a circle. It's eternal with no beginning and end, just a transformation from one form to another. Mandala confines to a circular boundary where there is no start, no culmination but only a DOT right in the center to make us aware of our consciousness. Carl Jung, the renowned name associated with Mandala expertise, described it as "a representation of the unconscious self."

The Mandala is a symbol that represents the Universe. The Universe is within the Self-Consciousness of our inner being, with the outer world having no constraints, no boundaries. It gives us a sense of belonging, a safe space where accurate reflections can be created and understood. Mandala-making is both a reflective and a creative process.

It's a geometrical, graphical representation of a higher state of life or thought with a profound meaning revealing insights into our spiritual, emotional, and psychological state. The unique imagery created as a Mandala is nothing but a deeper reflection on the purpose of life, the true nature of oneself, the hidden deluge of emotions, and unwarranted thoughts. It's critical to self-understanding and self-acceptance (Carl Jung)—recognition of life's true mission and purpose with clarity of thoughts and calmness of a deluded mind.

Mandala is a means to set off some of these erratic behaviors occurring within a body, sometimes unconsciously and often unconsciously. It's a tool to bring order to the disbalance of emotions because life's daily inevitable struggles and challenges must be conquered and surmounted with joy, happiness, and belief. Mandala reaffirms the positive mind and brings calm to the chaos within.

Mandala is a representation of wholeness and completeness. It symbolizes being one with life, reflecting inwards to the core and giving meaning to the emotions occurring within, directing them towards positivity and self-development.

The Mandala's Presence Since Time Immemorial

Our imagination is vast, wild, and wise. We are naturally attracted to shaped circles, spirals, and round objects because of an inner urge to connect to an entity. Primitive-aged people had a close connection with circular shapes recurring in their environment. The Sun, The Moon, and The solar system moved in an orbit. These circular movements' changes were the basis for critical decisions in historic and pre-historic times, much visible on the faces of rocks and caves in circular shapes. Over time, varied religions emerged that hovered around the Sun, a symbol representing energy and life: Sun Gods and goddesses symbol of worship for well-being, protection, and longevity. Circular drawings started appearing in performing religious rituals across myriad cultures and sects. Circular depictions started to show visibility on floors and walls with different materials like colored sand., dried spices, herbs, and natural colors made from flowers and petals.

To date, cultures from all directions use such complex geometrical representations as religious symbols in the healing and creative process. In the North America Navajo, sand drawing Art is made on the floor to perform secret religious ceremonies. In India, Mandalas, Kolam, and Alpana are drawn with rice flour, spices, and colored grains to honor Gods and bring home prosperity. Tibet is the hub of the West, where Sand mandalas are a weeks-long process made for self-awakening and symbolically erasing the Art after completion to illustrate and mark the impermanence of life. Australian culture is known to make use of 'Aborigines' as sand drawings made to establish a connection with the deceased ancestors in dreams.

The nature of Mandalas, whether Cult or Personal, defines its scope and flow. Cult Mandalas, mainly prominent in India and Tibet, have a pre-defined structure and style with deep-rooted symbols and motifs that give meaning and essence to their creation. On the other hand, Personal Mandalas broaden the horizon of the sacred space as there is no restriction on the kind of pattern, motif, or symbol used while making it. It represents an individual's Universe and personal experiences with the outer world. Intuition and instinct are the basis for the mandala creation. Its basic form is meditative and aims to bring a meaningful transformation in an individual's thought process, perceptions, and being.

It doesn't matter from which zone the Mandala originates. Whether it's an entirely intuitive process or is constructed within the defined cult boundaries. The motifs or symbols any Mandala entails are archetypal. The Father of Mandala interpretation and psyche, Carl Gustav Jung, introduced the Mandala subject to the Western world in the early 1900s. His day would mainly start by sketching symmetrical circular patterns in his famous journal known as the "Red Book." He wanted to get an insight into his inner emotional being. His findings pointed towards one aspect, which is "one's core." Awakening of the Self' was his most significant finding through creating Mandalas.

Spread of Mandalas Across Cultures

The existence of Mandalas is deeply rooted in many prevalent cultures across the globe. The primary roots of where Mandala has its widespread are Hinduism and Buddhism. Vedas were the first literature about mandalas, around 1500-500 BC. The Buddhist monks, however, are found to travel to the regions outside India. They were accountable for the spread of Art across America, Japan, China, Korea, Indonesia, America, and Tibet.

Science has evidence of Circular Symmetry found in phylogenetic mandalas. Not leaving the archaeological sites, the presence of the Mandala gets to reflect in the valley of Manipur, India, constructed with the aid of GoogleEarth imagery. The world's probable largest Mandala is the "Maklang geoglyph "in Imphal. Spread over 224,161.45 square meters, This gigantic Mandala square-shaped has four identical rectangular 'gates' in the four cardinal directions. The square entails an eight-petalled flower or rayed star named Maklang' Star Fort' spread over a total area of around 50,836.66 square meters. The five giant mandalas discovered, namely the Sekmai mandala, Heikakmapal mandala, Phurju twin mandalas, and Sangolmang mandala, are placed on the western bank of the Iril River. Nongren Mandala and Keinou mandala in the Manipur Valley are nature's gifts to humankind.

Mandala represents a political model in the 20th century adopted by Western historians from Asian Indian polities. Bagan, Ayutthaya, Champa, Khmer, Srivijaya, and Majapahit empires were called "mandala" in traditional Southeast Asian political formations.

Hinduism

Ancient Hinduism reveals Mandala as a Yantra. A yantra is a fair representation with four T-shaped doors meeting at an intersection or a central point. It's a spiritual geometric composition used for meditative, ceremonial purposes and is considered a holy place for the abode of the deity. For instance, widely revered in Hinduism is the Sri Yantra, created by Lord Shiva and used for worshipping, devotion, and meditation. It aims to attract all the positive energies and maintains harmony and balance in the home and workplace. It's also believed that Lord Shiva gave the world 64 chakras and their mantras to gain varied spiritual and material benefits. The yantra embodies the tri-energy of the cosmos, The earth, the Atmosphere, and the Sun. The yantra represents a total of nine interlocking triangles. With a focal point in the center, four triangles point upwards, representing Lord Shiva, and the remaining five points downward, representing Shakti.

Also used for Tantric practices, yantra symbolizes the man's connection with the outer spiritual forces. The macrocosm of the outer Universe gets fused with the microcosm of the individual's entity. Mandala appears as a Navagraha representation of the cosmos in the Vedic rituals.

Buddhism

Mandalas in Buddhism are more inclined towards meditative and spiritualist practices. We enter the Mandala by focusing on the central point. This process helps in transforming oneself from suffering to joy. Mandalas are spread widely over various Buddhist cultures and different sects. For instance, In "Tibetan Buddhism "Mandala is a symbolic representation of the entire Universe.

In this same sect, Mandala is an offering to the teacher or the Buddhas for their services regarding the training of the monks.

In Tibetan culture, sand mandalas have a very distinguished history, still in practice symbolizing the impermanence of life. They create a mandala on a floor surface with different materials such as grains, colors, etc. Monks make intricate representations in sand art, ultimately destroyed by sweeping away the powder or the grains and collecting them in an urn and later releasing the contents in a flowing river. The act represents that life is a flowing river, and nothing remains forever.

In Theravada Buddhism, mainly, different Mandalas are featured as part of the Pali Buddhist texts. Such as Mandala representing Buddha's Eight Disciples spread in eight different directions and Shakyamuni Buddha being placed right in the center. Many more variations of such kind are visible in Theravada Buddhism mandalas.

Apart from nature, Mandala representations are prominent in the field of architecture. Buddhist architectures, mainly temples and stupas, have a spell bounding complex Mandala-inspired designs that make a person awestruck by their beauty and creativity. Borobudur in Central Java, Indonesia, is an architecture that stands tall, immersed in its mesmerizing beautiful art structure, a magnanimous tantric Buddhist mandala. Other famous examples are the Sewu, Plaosan, and Prambanan. Mandala architectural monuments are also observable in Cambodia, Thailand, and Myanmar.

Nichiren Buddhism

In Nichiren Buddhism, Mandala is a scroll representation called a moji-mandala. It's a scroll of paper hanging over a wooden tablet inscribed in Chinese characters and medieval-Sanskrit script. The Mandala or the scroll represents the life state of Nichiren Daishonin, who believed that every individual is a Buddha. The Mandala is called the Gohonzon, inscribed by the founder, Nichiren Daishonin Buddhism, somewhere in the 13th century. The Gohonzon is the supreme object of devotion. The seven characters of "Nam-myoho-renge-kyo "in the Mandala or the scroll represent the world of Buddhahood inherent in one's own life and in all living or sentient things. The scroll or the Mandala can evoke the latent limitless potential inherent in every individual. "Kosen-Rufu or World Peace" and "Human Revolution" are the basis of the spiritual practice which teaches that all people are Buddhas. He then expressed it in the Gohonzon as a focus for Buddhist practice. Nichiren Daishonin awakened to this law and said, "I, Nichiren, have inscribed my life in sumi ink, so believe in the Gohonzon with your whole heart. The Buddha's will is the Lotus Sutra, but the soul of Nichiren is nothing other than Nam-myoho-renge-kyo" (WND-1, 412).

The Emergence and Perpetuation of Mandala in the Western Culture

The presence of mandala art reflects in their architecture. The cathedrals and Churches, in particular, were built with symbolic and emblematic Art and stained glassed windows, also known as "rose windows," constructed in the form of Mandalas. The rose is a symbol of passion, love, and compassion. This symbol was represented through a window, symbolizing the divinity, the unison of the cosmic energies, and the blessings of the creator. The Art and the architecture of the West represented the mandala art in beautiful tapestries, ceiling designs and patterns, engraved symbols, carved wooden Art, and other art forms. People used round illustrations for spiritual practices that resembled the modern mandalas of the century today.

The presence of the Mandala art form is visible in Christianity in the condition of the Cosmati pavements. These are geometric Mandala designs at Westminster Abbey, probably in the 13th century. Other representations of Hildegard von Bingen are also examples of the Mandala's prevalence in the culture. The Sigillum Dei, or the Seal of God, is a famous geometric depiction made by mathematician and astrologer John Dee is another evidence of the Mandala's existence since early times.

The Navajos sand paintings in North America resembled mandala art with a grand purpose of creation in the olden times. These creations serve as a formal healing process in which the sick person is seated in the center of the sand painting to carry on the healing process. The process was time-consuming and secretive. Hence only a few people knew about it. Such images centered around a midpoint stretched out in four directions.

The Native Americans use Mandalas as a symbol of prosperity, good luck, happiness, and harmony. It's the cycle of life, birth, and death. It's an amalgamation of man, nature, and spirituality in a circular form. In Native North America, the term Medicine wheel, also referred to as stone monument, medicine mountain is an allegory for spiritual and healing tribal practices. The medicine wheel symbol was a means to portray numerous expressions, mainly a National Historic Monument in 1970. The Medicine Wheel is a circular embodiment of limestone emboldens. It measures 80 feet in diameter with 28 rock spokes scorching from a center stone waymark.

The reinventing of the mandalas or the continuance of the Mandala connect in modern Western culture is all due to the incredible efforts of the great psychologist Carl Gustav Jung. In his quest to unveil the unconscious Self, past research reveals that drawings created within a circular boundary reflect the state of mind in the moment of creation. C.G.Jung termed the circular pictures a 'Mandala' after establishing facts through intense research and exploring the subject. He discovered that "Mandala is the Self, the Wholeness of the personality, which if all goes well is harmonious" (Carl Jung, Memories, Dreams, Reflection, pp, 195-196.) Carl propelled the need for mandala creation in times of discovering or re-discovering oneself to maintain harmony and balance within one's core. The research carried out by Carl Jung was further validated and strengthened by American art therapists Joan Kellogg and David Fontana.

Chapter – 03

MANDALA AND SYMMETRY

I often wondered why a soul is naturally attracted to patterns: Flowers, Nature, Universe, Celestial bodies, and Architecture, to name just a few. I could spend hours absorbing nature's bestowed symmetrical and asymmetrical patterns that extended an unspoken calm to a restless, chaotic mind and body. My erratic emotions come to a halt when I see a butterfly hovering from one end to another, playing mischievously in her symmetric colorful attire, or when I see the daunting mountain ranges arranged in an ordinal pattern, unfurling layer after layer, their courage and unbeatable strength. A snowflake dropping down from the arms of the sky is waiting to get embraced in safe hands. A sunflower stands tall in its mesmerizing beauty, knowing that every day the dusk compels him to hide on his shelf but still eagerly waits to bloom with the radiance of the sunshine, saying, "Hello! It's time to rise again". Symmetry evokes peace, harmony, courage, hope, gratitude, appreciation, inner calm, and resolves to bounce back amidst life's trials and tribulations. Fruits, Flora, Fauna, Human cells, Tree rings, Solar system, Galaxies, Celestial bodies, Ripples in the water, Echo of sounds, etc., are just a few examples of natural organic Mandalas in our environment surrounding us.

The archeology of structures has a long embraced history of Mandala in their layouts. Often we come across the design of cities, villages, labyrinths, buildings, and ancient monuments highly influenced by Art.

Symmetry is everywhere. The almighty's creation of a human form is the most prominent example of a symmetric creation, making us understand its purpose of harmony, integration, and coherence. Two eyes, one nose, two nostrils, two hands, two legs, one heart, and all other organs working in tandem and order to maintain perfect harmony, but what if? This harmony gets disrupted, the order gets distorted, and chaos, turbulence, and a commotion occurs within that reflects outside in various forms. Critical illness, mental ill health, distress, disharmony, frustration, and physical fatigue are common residues of these imbalances. Our body is controlled to a great extent by our mind. So when the reason is at ease, even the most challenging times are easy to sail through.

Mandalas show us the path whereby 'we can master our minds rather than the mind master us.' Mandala and Symmetry go hand in hand; they are two sides of the same coin. Sometimes, when we get stuck with Symmetry, the easiest way to break the monotony is to go Asymmetrical. ***Breaking boundaries is also necessary to know the worth of confinement.***

Soulful Symmetries Existing within A Mandala

Technically there are types of symmetries present take around us. A Mandala exhibits three kinds of symmetric patterns.

- **Bilateral Symmetry:** Symmetry that rests on a central axis. Observe a butterfly with her wings wide open. Bilateral Symmetry, when divided from its central axis, produces a mirror image.

- **Radial Symmetry:** Radial Symmetry is where or also known as 'Reflective Symmetry,' where a line is drawn through the image at some part of it, and the shape reflected on the other side is just a mirror image of the earlier one. Reflective Symmetry focuses on a central point. Imagine a starfish, coral, or maybe a slice of a Kiwi fruit. They all have a radial symmetry where the focus lies in the center, eventually radiating outwards. The line of reflection in a Mandala is that line that divides the Art into two mirror-image shapes. If the Mandala needs to be folded, the image reflecting along the line of its reflection will line up seamlessly.

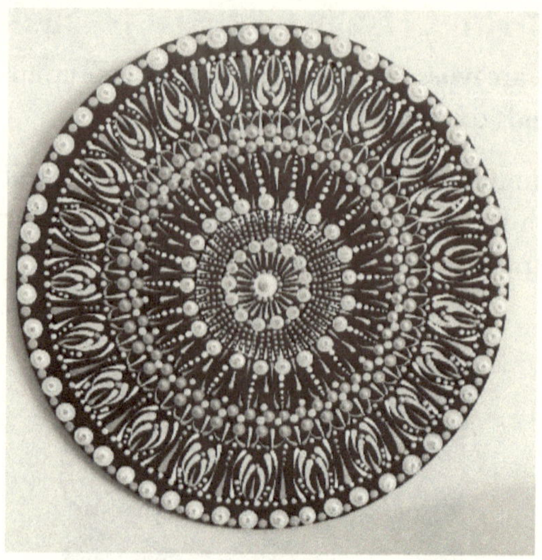

> **Rotational Symmetry**: The symmetry one observes while spinning the Mandala and repeatedly seeing the same patterns. The 'angle of rotational symmetry or also known as the 'angle of symmetry' is the smallest angle by which one can rotate the image to generate an identically oriented figure.

Any intuitively drawn meditative mandala divided into a certain number of orders or parts with repetitive patterns is an example of rotational Symmetry.

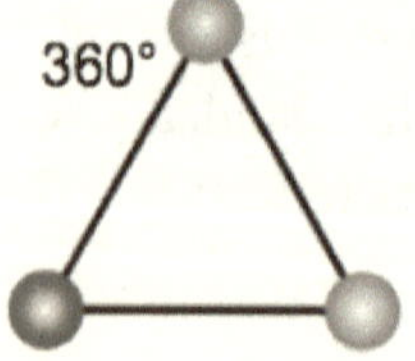

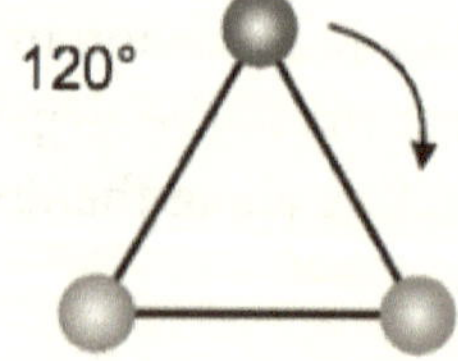

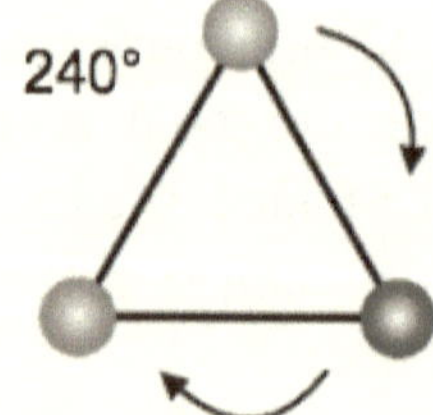

Draw a Perfect Symmetrical Mandala

Getting the circle's center right is a prerequisite to a perfect symmetrical Mandala. There are quite a few methods to achieve the same.

Method 1

1. Draw a line anywhere on the circle. It's called a Chord.

2. Find the midpoint of this chord by using a ruler.

3. Make a 90-degree angle using this midpoint and draw a straight line.

4. Draw another chord.

5. Repeat steps 2 and 3.

6. Draw more chords for accuracy if you like.

7. The point of intersection of the different chords gives you the circle's center.

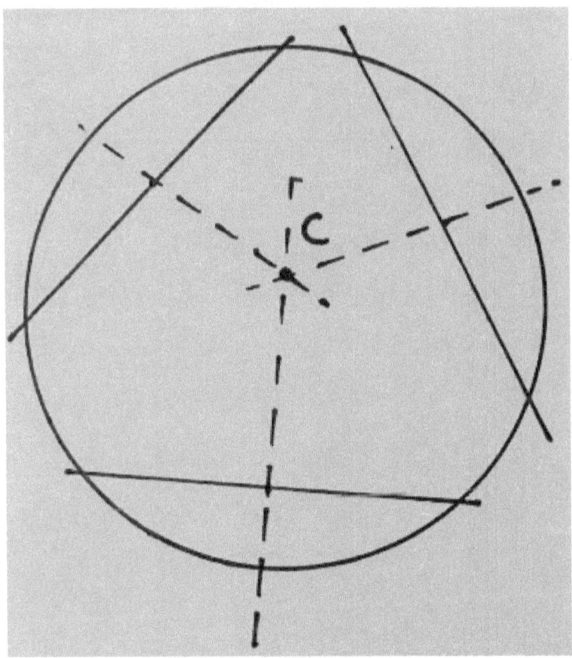

Method 2

1. Draw a circle.

2. Sketch a chord between two points, AB

3. Sketch another parallel chord CD with the same length as off AB.

4. Join AC and BD.

5. The point of intersection is the center of the circle.

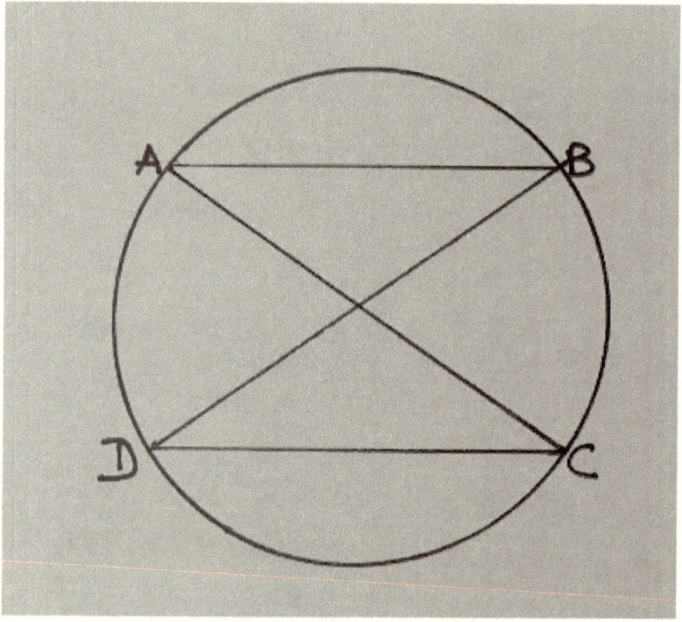

Method 3

1. Mark two straight, intersecting tangent lines onto the circle.

2. Draw tangent lines on the other side of the circle as well.

3. The four tangents together form a parallelogram.

4. Sketch a diagonal for the parallelogram drawn above.

5. The point of intersection is the center of the circle.

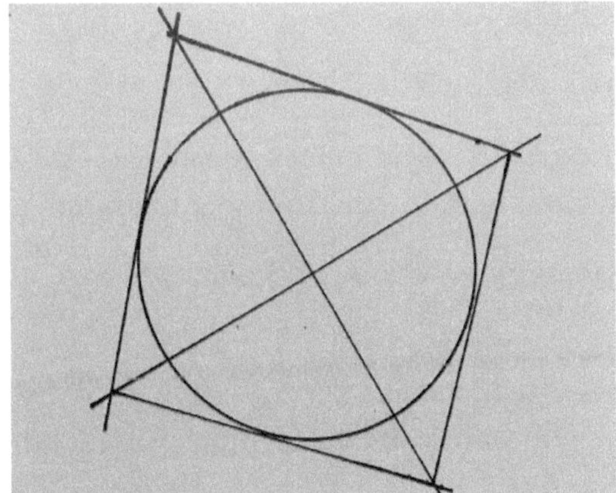

Order of Rotation

Every Mandala has a certain number or order of Symmetry derived from its rotation angle. The order of rotational Symmetry is the total number of positions in which a Mandala rotates and still appears the same as before the rotation. For instance, a mandala has five as its order of Symmetry, hence can have five times rotation, and with every course, it looks identical.

1. Every circle has a 360° angle.

2. The smallest angle by which we can rotate the Mandala to produce an identical configuration is 45°.

Hence, the order of rotation is 360°/45°= 8

The total order of SymmetrySymmetry of an object is the sum of the order of rotational Symmetry and the equal number of its lines of reflection.

Order of Symmetry = Order of Rotational Symmetry + Lines of Reflection

When we rotate the Mandala to get the same image, we have eight lines of reflection and eight charges of total Symmetry. Hence the entire order of Symmetry comes out to 8 + 8 = 16.

45°

MANDALA AND ITS TYPES

Since ancient times and in varied cultures, Mandala has held a promising position regarding its meaning, purpose, and intent. An 'Outer Mandala,' as it's called, represents the Universe as a whole, mainly used as an offering or thanking gesture in Buddhism.

Three main types of Mandalas are found in various cultures existing since centuries ago.

Teaching Mandala

Mandalas are a source for instructional and educational purposes where every shape, line, and color has a distinct meaning to religious beliefs and systems. Christianity, Hinduism, or Buddhism, teaching Mandalas, were constructed and designed to reflect their value system and principles. Monks mainly carried Mandalas as instructional tools or colorful mental maps. A person who created this kind of Mandala poured his holistic learning of a spiritual journey through visual acuity.

Healing Mandala

A meditative, therapeutic, or Healing Mandala arouses a Zen-like aura and curbs the negative emotions arising within a restless soul seeking peace, calm, composure, and wisdom. These insightful Mandalas, typically intuitive, also aided in enhancing concentration, attention, and focus while working with the creators understanding and capturing of self-expression. These spiritual Mandalas are symmetric to promote harmony and mindfulness. Clarity of thoughts and letting go of entangled emotions are by-products one can gain from practicing a healing mandala.

Sand Mandalas

Traditional, religious Art made from colored sand, drawn on the floor, usually prevailed and still exists in the Tibetan and Navajo culture marking the fundamental law of impermanence of human life. It's a belief that monks diligently and consistently work on a piece of Art for twelve consecutive days, giving the creation the minutest touches and spell bounding intricacies, all with the sand powder using metal and a small tube. The purposeful enticing Art is magnanimously created only to be erased on the thirteenth day. The leftover is collected in an urn and released in the flowing water.

The Mandala symbolizes that every creation has a definite lifetime. Nothing lasts forever. It's all in the 'moment.' The past has to be gone, the future is unseen, but the present is the moment of existence. Live your core in every moment of your existence.

Sand Mandala or Rangoli in India

India is a land of rich, diversified cultures grounded in spirituality. The reflection of age-long Sand Mandalas is eminent in the Rangoli or Rangavalli art is prevalent in various states of India. Rangoli means 'array of colors" in Sanskrit. However, the objective or purpose of sketching a sand mandala on the floor or entrance of homes, temples, and religious places is the same. The Art is created with an auspicious intent to bring prosperity, good luck, joy, and wealth to the family and welcome gods and Goddesses to bless the dwelling. Especially on festive days, essential occasions like a wedding in the house, Rangoli is considered auspicious. In many Hindu households, creating Rangoli art is an everyday practice. People make exquisite designs, mostly with bare fingers, using sandstone powder, flowers, or grain flour.

Apart from being just a decorative art, Rangoli serves as a 'Panch Mahabhoota Seva' because the material used for creating it is a feed to ants and other insects. Rangoli is referred with different names in different states of India' Kolam' in Tamil Nadu, 'Mandana in Rajasthan,' 'Alpana' in West Bengal, 'Aripana' in Bihar, 'Muggulu' in Andhra Pradesh, 'Aipan' in Uttarakhand and 'Jhoti' in Orissa.

Rangoli holds a striking resemblance with Sand Mandala art differing in one critical aspect, which is the purpose of creation. Rangoli is a decorative art made to bring good fortune and happiness to the household. At the same time, Sand Mandala is a graphical geometric representation of the spiritual Universe and its myriad realms. While It takes weeks to finish one Sand Mandala, Rangoli is an everyday practice in many Indian households.

Chapter – 05

MANDALA MAKING, A SOULFUL PROCESS

While creating a Mandala rejuvenates the soul, moving forward toward an astute journey. Still, following the undermentioned pointers can undoubtedly help in extracting the maximum benefits out of the process of connecting with one's unconscious mind.

1. Be mentally prepared to sit for at least an hour for the creation to shape up. Make sure the primary material required is ready before the session. (pencil, ruler, compass, paper, pen, colors, etc.)

2. Take a deep breath and try to calm your mind and body.

3. Pick up your journal and write down your thoughts, whatever they may be.

4. Post your writing, Park all your thoughts for the moment, and try to live that moment consciously with yourself with a blank mind.

5. Get the focus on your inner core, reflecting and meeting yourself.

6. Begin by putting a 'DOT' in the center. It is the representation of your inner consciousness with the outer world.

7. Sketch a cross through the dot to create four quadrants. Further, divide these quadrants into eight equal parts, making the order of Symmetry. It can extend into 16 orders to create a mirror image and rotational Symmetry.

8. Take a few moments to be aware of your consciousness, reflect on the segments created, and focus on the dot in the center.

9. Be comfortable, avoid distractions, put on soulful music, or light some scented candles. Enjoy the process and live your core; evolve and set your inner feelings into patterns, colors, and shapes. Here an intuitive, free-flowing mandala will reflect the real emotions hidden inside.

10. Once you completed your Mandala, you have created a safe space for yourself; revisit your Mandala as it represents your inner Self. Let the center be your focal point and move outwards. Layer by layer, you are unveiling your emotions. Again, pick up your journal and write what you feel about the Self you created. Be honest with your feelings and thoughts while writing.

11. Observe the changes Self underwent from the beginning to after writing your journal.

Chapter – 06

BENEFITS OF PRACTICING MANDALA ART

A wandering mind needs stillness to become aware and adapt to the changing environment around us. The ultimate goal of practicing the Mandala art form is a perfect sync between body, mind, and soul. Awakening of the spiritual Self is an inconspicuous benefit one experiences while making or even coloring a Mandala. Recognition of Self, healthy and unhealthy thoughts and behaviors, clarity of thoughts, and release from Self-built confinements are a few generic recompenses for practicing Mandala art.

Enhances Focus

Consistently working on patterns, detailing, coloring, and creating Symmetry brings calm to a restless, galloping mind, creating harmony between Self and the environment. A peaceful mind has a longer attention span and focus.

In children, Mandalas helps to enhance visualization skills. Cognitive growth is one of the substantial benefits of practicing Mandala Art. Coloring Mandalas at an early age boosts creativity, imagination, and concentration. Eye-hand coordination enhances with regular practice.

Retention

Concentration on the Dot and engaging with regular repetitive patterns can also aid in strengthening and honing retention skills. It's a healthy exercise for brain functioning; strengthening the brain's right hemisphere enhances creativity and short-term memory.

Reduces stress

Stress has become our unwanted companion in our life's journey. Relationships, health, or finances are key trigger points to stress, which, if not managed consciously and efficiently, leads to severe life imbalances and disharmony within the five elements of the human body. Creating Mandala or coloring Mandala brings back the order to lead a balanced life. It helps control emotions, thereby calming a strained self and surroundings.

Children are going through a turmoil of emotions in the present-day scenario. Peer pressure, personal and parental expectations, Image building, society acceptance, etc., can all build emotional disharmony within. Coloring Mandala or drawing patterns can help young minds to reduce their anxiety and emotional disorder.

Instills Confidence

For adults and children who lack confidence and are hesitant to express their hidden emotions, Mandalas can be of great benefit. Creativity, originality, recognition of Self-worth enhances confidence. Control of the mind brings in control over negative and deterring thoughts. They learn to break patterns and accept changes.

Transformation

One of the most fruitful results of Mandala undertaken as an art therapy is a complete transformation of Self. From a place of helplessness to a wiser, confident, and awakened identity, Mandala aids in transforming human sufferings and unpleasant emotions into joy and happiness. From an ordinary being to an enlightened soul, Mandalas transform negative human emotions into positive, hopeful affirmations and actions.

Therapeutic for Special Needs

Mandala Art works wonders when it aims to serve the needs of special kids and adults challenging autism, ADHD, Asperger Syndrome, etc., to name a few. Challenging day-to-day life chores can be overwhelming and add to physical and mental fatigue. For special needs, the diversified areas where Mandala art can benefit are:

- Strengthening of gross and fine motor skills in children and adults. Different art techniques, such as 'pointillism,' coloring, crafting, etc., can be used.

- Eye-hand coordination

- Focus

- Concentration

- Increased attention span

- We are introducing Conceptual knowledge of boundaries, colors, geometric shapes, patterns, etc.

- Muscle toning and strengthening

- Reduced hyperactivity

Mandala art, when taken up as a therapeutic intervention, can bring a lot of calmness, relaxation, and peace for differently abled all age groups. It can be vocational training for a few who are interested in Art. The mandala art, along with other art forms, can explore the talent of special needs individuals helping them to make a livelihood out of the recreational activity.

Aid to Clinical Intervention

With the rising complexities of the modern era, extreme work pressures, strained relationships, compromised value systems, and a fast lifestyle, there is a sudden surge in the number of people suffering from acute depression and anxiety disorders. However, the main course of treatment for such mental and emotional ailments is through clinical diagnosis and medical intervention. Yet, art therapy, including Mandala Art, when combined with medical treatment, can work as a catalyst for the cure and well-being of the patient. Such treatment can lead to faster positive results as an individual gets a chance to know thy Self and introspect within without fearing being judged and prejudiced. The side effects of the spiritual intervention are negligible, and the probability of positive results is high in patients undergoing a dual practice of medical and spiritual healing compared to people who opt only for clinical intercession. Past clinical studies prove that Mandalas have helped improve patients' immune systems, lowering and stabilizing blood pressure and regularizing erratic sleep patterns.

Chapter – 07

EFFICACY OF A DOT

A Dot is a minimal symbol to represent a universe within. The simplest element in art represents wholeness and completeness. A dot right in the center of the Mandala is nothing but 'self.' The Self comes into being through the spiritual, psychological, and emotional aspects of one's life. The dot represents the amalgamation of the inner consciousness with the outer form. We create a structure based on our perceptions, beliefs, and experiences. A Dot reflects our consciousness without holding any boundaries or constraints.

According to Carl Jung, creating a Mandala was to get closer to that 'Dot,' which is nothing but the Self. Mandala allows us to realize our unhealthy thoughts and behaviors, thereby Self-accepting our individuality, leaving behind irrational illusions that create one's psychological vision and notions.

A dot or center is free from all dimensions, with no beginning or end. It's a minimal symbol of representation of the start, process, and back. Patterns and symbols in the orbit of a dot represent the cosmos, which ensembles with the outer circle to reflect the repetitive vicious nature of our life.

Apart from the importance of the existence of a Dot in Mandala and related art forms, a Dot also has various other implications. For writers, a Dot marks the end of a sentence. Musicians put Dots to compose soulful melodies. Dot marks the unmanifested. Connecting dots helps to place the right puzzle pieces and solve complexities and entangled emotion. Randomly expressed dots after penning down words express continuity, scope for more, expression of revealing the unsaid, unworded emotion....

Chapter – 08

HOW TO START A MANDALA FROM A 'DOT'?

A dot is a representation of a universe. The center or the focal point of a Mandala is the core. There are two ways to create a Mandala.

1. From the outer circle moving inwards towards the center/core

2. From the center, moving outwards towards the inner and the outer layer

A Mandala that moves from the center outward will release all its hidden energies, positive and negative, along its journey. These emotions are likely to be wanting to manifest in outer space. A core that seeks validation and acceptance in the outside world can be its true worth through Mandala Art.

A mandala that moves inwardly tries to finds its core values by shedding all its layers and then finding its soul purpose of life. The mission which is unique, a purpose that is the reason for one's existence and attaining absolute happiness.

Chapter – 09

MANDALA MAKING: A PROCESS

Mandala creation is a delicate process for a curious, inquisitive soul. There are no rules, constraints, or regulations controlling making any mandala. A process here in a mandala creation doesn't only aim to create a perfect symmetric piece of Art. Instead, it is a means to explore our inner Self. Our inner realm sometimes resists showing its actual state. Mandala creation, whether done from a reflective perspective or a creative aspect, tends to tap our core and allows us to 'Live our Core' even briefly. As it's said, 'The only constant thing is Change itself". However, there is one prerequisite for a healing course: the presence of a circular boundary that also gives a sacred space for venting out our emotions. There are two ways to create a Mandala. Either we go as a 'Reflective Creative Process' or a "Creative Reflective Process." No matter which process we choose, the ultimate destination is a calm, relaxed, and higher state of life in a particular moment. We need to trust the process, surrender to it entirely and enjoy being a part of it.

Mandala Making: A Reflective Process

Life is tough. It's uncertain, unpredictable, and, many times, pretty harsh. Illness, marital discord, career setbacks, unfulfilled desires, chasing challenges one after another, loss of loved ones, personal crisis, identity crisis, foreign invasions, and wrath of nature are all circumstances of life that are part of our being. These are testing times of life to see our metal. Our ability to handle our life's difficult, tedious periods defines our true worth. We need to calmly control our random emotions that seem to lose direction and run haywire in all proximities for solutions but, unfortunately, mess up more.

Even if our inner entity is in a calm state of mind and has a balanced opinion of our momentary chaos, it's good to reflect upon our emotions. They may be unclear or not recognized to control the transitory phase of life. This situation is grave where emotions are trapped, wanting to be released but can hardly find a path to emancipation.

The inner calling is to get back to one's core, to attain a psychic balance. Reflective mandala-making can be the safest, most intuitive, most productive, and most creative way to find one's path to inner peace. Not surprisingly, random numbers of mandala seekers opt for such courses, retreats, workshops, and therapy classes to create conscious, reflective, meditative Mandalas for self-introspection, self-love, and self-awareness. Though the essential nature of the process begins with a reflection of our being as a whole, the method is creative. Gauging of central being is the prime upshot of a meditative mandala, along with Gratitude, Appreciativeness, Satisfaction, Fun, Enjoyment, and earning all as by-products of the same process.

It's a process to be thoroughly enjoyed and not taken as a course of therapy per se. It's experimental, fun, and a source of happiness without necessarily requiring any intervention from an external source. A round painted piece, a symmetrical drawing, or a little embroidered piece with different materials created impromptu without any que can be exhilarating and nourishing. Every art creation has a beautiful story, a unique universe waiting to be heard aloud, sometimes in words, other times in silence.

Reflection of the Soul

In the process, what do you reflect upon? It's the unconscious emotions that work inside out. It is an orchestra that creates a symphony between the inner microcosm of an individual with the macrocosm of the world outside. The Mandala serves as a focal point that reflects the psyche of an individual at a given moment. It represents itself in the form of shapes, lines, curves, colors, and patterns, which have a meaning to that very instant. Reflective Mandala making at this point is the process of assimilation of the inner deluge of information and transformation of the same into a mandala. This process can be a real revelation of aspects in one's life that need immediate attention. Becoming aware of our hidden emotions can help heal a soul.

Reflective should always be encouraged as an intuitive exercise, not a directed one. A mandala, if copied or instructed, can lead to false conclusions. Many times, the emotions that are finding an opportunity to flow get suppressed. A reflective Mandala mainly shapes up through one's thoughts and inner urges.

But suppose people restrain themselves entirely during the initial process. In that case, the thought of putting something on paper makes them more anxious, then merely coloring a pattern can also help lower anxiety. Colors, shapes, or practices don't need an immediately visible relation to our core. It requires consistency to bring real meaning to the content created. Emotions are of all types, ranging from positive to unpleasant ones. They all should be allowed to flow freely; then, only can they be transformed in the desired course.

By making an outer layer and filling it with whatever emotions come up on the surface, an inside feeling can get a way out. Images that come on paper may make no sense initially, a crooked line, a clash, two opposite characters, a vague color scheme, numbers, or animal-looking shapes. Techniques are the factors that can enhance the pace or decrease the speed of the process. For instance, Mandala on paper with soft pastels will take less time than one drawn with acrylic colors or fine liner pens. Embroidery or very intricately drawn Art on wood or similar surface may take weeks or months to complete. The size and the intricacy will determine the time required for the process.

Any medium and technique may work effectively if no external intervention is required. If, on the other hand, expertise involvement is a part of the process, it's advisable to make more small-size mandalas with different color mediums for better interpretation and healing.

The book contains techniques and prerequisites to attain a meditative, reflective state. Try applying some of the basic techniques for an ecstatic experience.

Flow of Emotions

An individual goes through 3000 realms in a single moment of life. (the concept is explained further in the book). Emotions can be positive or negative. Sometimes positive emotions are emitted quite easily through shapes, patterns, and colors. Still, often, there is an inner resistance or conflict that makes the emancipation of emotions difficult. Under such scenarios, discomfort, distress, frustration, and withdrawal are expected behavior. Despite such episodes, one should be encouraged to carry on. These are the areas that need attention. Once accepted, the healing process starts. It's not that every time creation of a mandala is a way for healing. Meditating and concentrating on the center of a mandala and reflecting on our thoughts that emerge on the surface can also be a good reflection of our inner emotions and feeling at that very moment.

Reflective Mandalas Don't Seek Perfection

The objectivity behind a meditative mandala is not to create a perfect symmetric pretty art. However; we are trying to bring harmony and peace to the existing imbalance between the inner and the outer Universe. Making Mistakes is a part of the process. It shows our actual state of subconscious being. Hence, let the flow be natural, absorbing discrepancies and imperfections. Let the process be all intuitive. Shapes, colors, patterns, and symbols must come out instinctively.

The analysis is not made on how perfectly the technicalities of the Art are incorporated but rather on the depth and ingenuity revealed in the complete process. Impromptu mandalas are best for reflective analysis without prior selection of any subject, topic, or cue. It helps in the reality check in a given moment of time frame. But if need be, universal subjects like elements of nature, numbers, characters, chakras, or likewise, can be used to interpret situations, such as personal relationships, financial issues, or health challenges.

Mandala Making: A Creative Process

Every individual is born creative. Do you agree with me? If yes, then great. If No, then think. Creativity is a part of us; it's only how much we use it in all fields and areas. Creativity is not just limited to Art, Craft, and Music. It's beyond the stereotypes we are born and nurtured with. Dance is one form of creativity. Many people learn classical music, which is the same for all, but only a few hold us and keep us intrigued with their expressions, aced movements, and the joy they bring into their performance. A simple example of creativity is a doctor giving an injection. Some make it so unbearable that it creates trauma for life. Still, few have the creativity to turn that painful task into a pleasant experience withdrawing all fears and phobias associated with it.

Creativity is a human urge or calls to depict thoughts, emotions, feelings, and to some extent, tasks in a way to make oneself understood. It's a method to put the non-verbal into a desired form. Creativity is a work of the soul and is unique to oneself. The degree of it may vary from person to person depending on the activation of the right or left hemisphere of the brain. Creation is spontaneous; at the spur of the moment, a feeling or intuition gets into shape or form.

As per scientific research, the two halves of our brains have their respective roles. While the left hemisphere is rooted more in analytical and logical screening, the right hemisphere inclines more toward non-verbal lexes, creativity, sexuality, spirituality, imagination, intuition, feelings, and emotions.

Since our childhood, our left brain has been in constant play. Learning, critical evaluations, making decisions based on logical facts, thinking, and overthinking all grow in the left hemisphere of our brain. All these tend to underplay our creative brain. The right brain is suppressed, clogged, and unused. When put to use equally to attain a balanced lifestyle, both aspects give better results. Hence we label people as artistic or analytical by nature.

But one should work on their weak hemisphere and strengthen it for healthy growth. A high-functioning left-brainer can tap into the creative zone by meditating, trying hands-on, accessible Art, and developing an interest in music or performing arts. While a high-functioning right-brainer can try to solve some logical and reasoning exercises, perform thought-provoking activities, easy model making, solve some case studies, etc.

It's not important what we do but the ichinen to do something to improve and work on ourselves constantly. However, at the same time, people who find the process quite overwhelming or are undergoing severe emotional outbursts and have been recommended clinical intervention must first seek medical advice. After a complete medical analysis and consent from their doctor, one can work with mandala structures and symmetric and geometric patterns; in such cases, releasing energy through physical stimulation is advised for maintaining harmony between the brain's left and right hemispheres.

Chapter – 10

JOURNALING

Journaling is the Art of recording personal thoughts, feelings, emotions, and insights in text, graphics, or pictures on paper or any other medium. Mandala is an outburst of emotions, both positive and negative. It's critical to know what one feels from moment to moment during the entire process. It would be of great help to pen down the same unbiased flow of emotions one goes through at the start and end of the process. Thoughts may be scattered, crumbled, or crystal clear. It's beautiful, whatever it may be. If a particular shape, pattern, color, form, or symbol is a preference of the subject, then it's crucial to write down the instincts behind that choice at that very moment. Such reflections can aid the healing process and confronting the fiend that needs our attention.

One may answer a few of the under-mentioned questions to journal their thoughts and analyze their inner emotional being through the medium of the Mandala. However, one must ensure that these questions are related to the moment when asked and reflected, not in a generic sense.

➢ Why did you choose a particular color, shape, or symbol at that very moment? What exactly crossed your mind during a specific selection?

➢ Why did you choose a particular subject, if any? Does the element you chose to represent your subject have a distinct meaning or relevance?

➢ What stopped you from being a part of a completely intuitive process? (applicable only when a particular subject is undertaken rather than being instinctual)

➢ What feelings did you experience right before the start of the Mandala? Were they chaotic, angry, calm, composed, or random?

- ▷ What feelings did you experience in the middle of the Mandala or at any other point that needs a mention? Were they chaotic, anxious, calm, composed, or random?

- ▷ During the process, did any pattern, color, symbol, or shape attract you the most towards it or cause resistance?

- ▷ Were you unperturbed while making mistakes or had a sudden urge to rectify them then and there?

- ▷ Did you deliberately evoke Symmetry in the Mandala, or it came naturally, or did you like it Asymmetrical?

- ▷ Any particular thought or incident that flashed instantly during the process?

- ▷ What feelings did you experience after the Mandala? Were they chaotic, anxious, calm, composed, or random?

These are a few guided questions; any feeling, gesture, or emotion evoked during the entire process must be written at any point that says something about an inner life state. Reflective mandalas eventually lead to unfurling our creative zone as well. Creations can sometimes surprise us, reflecting on areas and emotions we never considered worthy of mentioning. From such a deep, insightful journey, one can create his self-identity, which is momentary. We, humans, have no identical constant flow of thoughts. The results may be completely different and astonishing if the same process is reiterated for the same emotion but at another moment.

Chapter – 11

MANDALA TECHNIQUE TO ENHANCE THE CREATIVITY ZONE

To start with a simple mandala activity, one can choose to color the pre-available templates. Many kinds of stuff is available at various platforms and levels, from beginner to advanced. Choose as per your interest and attention span. Black and white mandalas can help stimulate creativity. Start by drawing a center, a focal point around which every unique Universe an individual creates revolves. In our minds, the generic pattern for a mandala is a circle with four or eight orders of Symmetry. The symmetric mandala design is a result of equal orders and creating repetitive patterns around the center. However, this is only sometimes the scenario with intuitive mandalas. Intuitive or reflective Mandalas may start with a circle but may end up in any shape oval, octagon, hexagon, or square. Such a creative Mandala emerges from the depths of one's life where the primary focus is creating, and reflection follows unconsciously.

Creative mandalas, in general, can be one of the following.

> It can be a circle with a center/focal point and a total order of Symmetry as 4 with symmetric repetitive patterns or abstract Art.

> It can be a circle with a center/focal point and a total order of Symmetry as 8 with symmetric repetitive patterns or abstract Art.

> It can be a circle with a center/focal point and a total order of Symmetry of 12 or more with symmetric repetitive patterns or abstract Art.

> It can be a circle with a center/focal point with an abstract or definite symmetric or asymmetric shape, symbol, or pattern.

> It can be a circle with no focal point but a concrete shape. It can be an animal figure, floral representation, or other symbol. The urge to create such a pattern or figure is spontaneous and based on an inner impulse at a given moment.

> Apart from a circle, any other shape can be pertinent, further divided into symmetric order of segments or asymmetric.

Pure Mandala

A circle with a fourfold symmetry/order of Symmetry or more is a pure mandala. The pre-requisite of a pure mandala is a circular boundary, a sacred or safe space for a unique universe. The center or the dot is the cosmos or one's higher state of life. The four orders or parts of the circle also represent the four cardinal directions, the four seasons, or the four main elements of nature in the human body (Air, Water, Fire, and Earth). However, some add a fifth element of 'Ether/Space.'

Few Effective Strategies for a Creative Mandala

Creativity has no bounds. Hence there are no rules and regulations to draw a particular pattern. Both symmetric and asymmetric, creativity can be explored and experimented with. Coloring a mandala can be the most leisurely start for a beginner to open his creative block and take the fest step toward his journey. Graduate oneself from coloring basic shapes to medium intricate patterns. Once the attention span is enhanced, high-level or highly complex designs can be opted for. From floral to figurative, all kinds of Mandala printed templates cater to individuals' interests. (do refer to my upcoming exclusive set of Mandala coloring books for a rejuvenating mindful experience)

Besides coloring, practical hands-on experience can be a positive outcome by adopting any strategy. The first alternative is to draw a mandala on a piece of Paper. Randomly choose the center of your Mandala as per instinct. Without using any tool like a ruler, compass, or protractor, start creating your Universe around the center or the focal point, and after that, make it as a whole. A pen liner or a gel pen can be used, preferably in black-on-white play. Gradually choose colors but limit them to three or four maximum initially. After that, when a few mandalas are tried and tested, expand your horizon and experiment with different colors and mediums. It's a creative process, so the focus should be to enjoy and be in the moment. Mistakes will happen, and it's part of the process, but with consistency and perseverance, patterns and thoughts will both gain clarity and sync.

The second alternative is to choose a paper with 180 gsm or above for strength and sturdiness. Mark the midpoints of the sheet, both vertical and horizontal. Wherever the points intersect is the center of the circle. Using a compass from the center, draw circles of various measurements randomly. Draw horizontal and vertical lines from the midpoint to create an order of Symmetry, 4, 8, 16, etc., from the center, and draw patterns radiating outwards. It's our inner self finding its way outwards. Once you choose a design, follow the same in all the sections created to give harmony and balance to your Universe. Here too, start with a few colors in a palette. Choose your color medium as per your inclination. Pencil colors, fine liner pens, soft pastel crayons, etc.; avoid using sketch pens as they can blotch and bleed, resulting in an unsatisfactory experience.

The third alternative is to find the 'focal point,' 'inner self,' and 'core' right at the end of the process. Draw a circular boundary on a sheet of Paper. Start filling it up with different shapes. One can use squares, triangles, rectangles, octagons, hexagons, etc. Create your world. A circular boundary helps to confine your Universe in a sacred safe space. Make use of creative patterns. Let your heart and soul be united in the process. Moving towards the inner layer from the outer layer and, on the way filling up your hidden layer will help you to assimilate various feelings. Emotions and thoughts lead you to your core values. It's a fascinating technique to break the repetitive patterns of our life, unleashing our creativity and thinking out of the box.

The fourth technique is creating a symmetric symbol that may or may not be circular. Here we focus on creating a radial symmetry rather than a rotational symmetry observed in alternative number two, as explained above. Radial Symmetry is one where a complete mirror-like image forms when cut from the center line of the Mandala. For instance, imagine the picture of the butterfly with its wings spread wide. Cutting it around a vertical line right from the center will result in a duplicate mirror-like pattern. We often find floral mandalas, animal-shaped mandalas like a lion, birds, butterflies, etc., depicting a radial symmetry. Here choose colors and mediums as per your inclination. Try on Different platforms or surfaces to experience novelty and creativity.

The fifth technique uses dots as a pattern all over right, from choosing the center to filling the inner and outer layers. A pre-defined structure in the form of equally divided sections and circles can help to ace this technique called a 'Dot Mandala.' Dotting tools are readily available in the market. They give us the freedom to choose dots of different sizes.

For people who don't have professional dotting tools, the material available in our homes can be a valuable source for plotting dots. A pencil with a flat end can make perfect dots. Toothpicks, sticks, ear bud or any other available tool can create dots of various sizes. Here we generally make use of paints, acrylic, or poster paints. Ensure the consistency of color, not too fluid or thick; else, the dots won't appear deftly. Try Dot Mandala on various surfaces, such as Paper, wood, canvas, glass, and acrylic sheets are a few bases to try upon.

The sixth technique fuses dot patterns with other geometric shapes and subjects. One can use dotting tools, paint brushes, textured tools, and other creative mediums here. Labyrinths, spirals, and Celtic knots, to name a few, are different creations that broaden our horizons and rekindle our analytical insights through the mandala-making process. There is no end to how intricate one can make such a creative art form. It all depends on the subject one decides upon, the mental being of an individual, and the surface one chooses. As the above-mentioned alternative strategies explain, the process and color medium remains the same.

After creating a beautiful, unique Universe of your own through any of the above techniques, it's best to hang them in a visible and radiating place. Constantly gazing and looking at the Mandala itself is comforting and can help in a more profound reflection or introspections emotions will erupt by looking at the same Mandala each time with a different perspective. If you make a variety of them, you can change them frequently depending on mood swings, color combinations, pattern connections, etc. Gifting your handmade creation is the most self-satisfactory feeling. Mandalas can be framed and mounted or stored in folders for future perusal.

Chapter – 12

MATERIAL REQUIRED FOR MAKING MANDALA

While reflective Mandalas don't require much material, just paper and a pen to start with. Once the connection with the art forms gradually, one can increase the level of difficulty too and try to experiment with different mediums and techniques. A creative Mandala, however, has no bounds. Aesthetics, also part of the process, requires selective use of the mediums. Under mention is a list of available materials recommended for creating different types of mandalas with unique patterns and styles.

1. Paper

2. Pen (Black fine liners, gel pens, markers)

3. Colored pens

4. Oil pastels

5. Soft/chalk pastels

6. Charcoal pencils

7. Pencil colors

8. Watercolors

9. Oil paints

10. Acrylic paint

11. Compass

12. Protractor

13. Ruler

14. Pencil

15. Eraser

16. Paint Brushes

17. Dotting tools

18. Wooden Board

19. Canvas

20. Fabric

If you have already worked with all or a few mentioned mediums, their pros and cons must already be clear to you. Hence, the selection of the material becomes easy. However, if you are an amateur, then all the better. The experience of using colors and trying to connect with the process is very satisfying, intriguing, and exciting. There will be little goofs and ups, mistakes, learning, and a spurt of creativity. Have fun and experiment. Don't obstruct your inner self with technicalities. Consistency and practice will naturally enhance efficiency, productivity, and confidence.

Chapter – 13

MANDALAS BEYOND PAPER

Mandalas are not only restricted to Paper. Pen Mandalas, especially in black and white, is one of the most common and productive but not the only ones. Different techniques can be tried and tested on Paper as well. For instance, one can create textures by applying water on a wet-on-wet surface to give a colorful base to a Mandala. Different textures can be created through acrylic/poster paints on Paper, making a mandala universe. Stencils are an excellent medium to paint pre-mark designs on Paper and other base materials to outline your Mandala.

MDF materials are widespread and trendy these days. Exploring different color types and shapes of various sizes and patterns on the MDF base is enticing. Ultimately, one can get a glossy or a matt finish to your by varnishing it with readily available spray or liquid. Acrylic paints are quick-drying paints that give quite room for correction if needed. However, oil colors take much time to dry and are only conducive to some weather conditions. Pen liners and brush pens are speedy tools with a smooth finish but give a small room for correction.

One can also try mandala patterns and fuse them with different art forms for an ultimate creative experience. I have attempted mandala fusion with Indian folk art, Madhubani, Kalamkari, and Warli art forms. The end product has been highly nourishing, giving a booster or a kickstart to the thought process and flow of emotions.

Macrame mandalas

Macrame is the Art of knotting string in beautiful patterns to make exciting décor. Using colorful threads or standard white bases in macrame has a soothing effect on the mind and soul. People with an eye for Knitting can use this technique to create healing and creative Mandalas for themselves and others. These are very easy to maintain, highly portable and can be hung anywhere in the house or workspace adding to the aesthetics of the place as well.

Mandalas on Fabric

Making Mandala patterns on fabric is an exciting process. Fabric colors are readily available in the market. Emboss outlines and designs With the help of Stencils on the material for making fabric mandalas. People inclined towards such art forms can also create beautiful tapestries incorporating mandala art. Art on cloth can also be framed and used for meditation and healing of the soul. Mandala patterns are often trending, often imprinted on different attires—traditional suits, dupattas, stoles, shirts, sarees, etc., to name a few. Art here can also be turned into a source of livelihood, selling distinct unique patterns to designers and other creators. Applique or patchwork Mandalas can also be tried by turning swatches of cloth cut into geometric shapes and then sewn manually or by machine.

Clay Mandalas or Healing Art

Clay art is an ancient Egyptian art form where beautiful, breathtaking Art is created through textural or cone work using cement powder, plaster of Paris, marble dust powder, chalk powder, etc.; generally done on walls, wood, and Cardboard, this Art aimed to create 3D objects. Mandala art can be fused very well into this art form to create some fantastic sculptures or Mandala art. The process is natural healing, bringing harmony to the chaos within a restless soul. People naturally get relaxed working with clay as a medium. We can significantly benefit by incorporating Mandalas with Cone art. it's time-consuming; it might take days, weeks, or even months to create a gorgeous, stunning piece of Art. This technique can significantly enhance attention span, focus, and eye-hand coordination. Because this medium is sensory and tactile, special needs children or adults can benefit a lot from this process as a whole. Circular harmony activates through clay art. These days super dry clay is an excellent medium to try with young age groups, keeping them engaged for an extended period and accentuating creativity.

Quill Mandalas

Paper art or quilling is one of the most enticing, time taking, focus-oriented Art. Creating gorgeous mandala patterns through the Art of quilling and using them for meditation or reflection is a creative, innovative exercise. It takes days and weeks to develop symmetrical quills in different patterns and sizes and finally assemble them to form a stunning symmetrical mandala. The fundamental objective is to unleash latent creativity to all extents possible. Such techniques enhance our perseverance and enduring traits that reflect our daily lives.

Floating/Floral Mandalas

Creating floral art (arranging flowers in various patterns) in water or floor, or other surfaces with additional adornments like scented floating candles, potpourri, sensor lights, etc., can be a meditative self-awakening healing process. People who feel good when surrounded by nature can often try this technique to bring calm and peace when anxious or irritated.

Embroidery Mandalas

Embroidery or cross stitch is another technique where Mandala making is well applied. Weaving intricate patterns and designs into a mandala using delicate beads of different sizes is not a day's work. It's a laborious, painstaking, and grueling task. Imagine hundreds and thousands of beads carefully woven to create small and big circular patterns. Eye-hand coordination, development of fine motor skills, and enhanced attention span are some advantages of applying this technique of mandala making. Cross stitch is also possible in fashioning some unique mandalas. The hidden, latent talents can fully bloom by exploring and challenging this specific art technique.

Crochet/Knit Mandalas

One may find beautiful eye-catching mandala patterns on various cloth types. Some may be knitted or crocheted by our highly talented grandmoms, who also reveal the art form's presence since immemorial. These handcrafted techniques are still persistent and more treasured when fewer people know such practices. Creating circular mandala patterns through this technique can be utterly soothing and comforting. These age-old techniques have a scientific advantage and bring harmony and balance to our confused and cluttered minds.

Woodcarving/ Metalwork Mandalas

Are Mandalas only limited to paper? Not. Magnificent creations of artistic galore exist in these handcrafted wood-carved Mandala patterns. The art itself leaves us spellbound. The symmetry and perfection displayed in this kind of art technique are commendable. Using tools for wood carving and metal work put extreme pressure on the hand, hence challenging. Getting perfection may consume a lot of time and requires endless patience. People who want to challenge themselves in learning different techniques while fusing those with Mandala making can try this art form and feel the difference.

Resin Mandalas

One of the most talked about art techniques of the current times is resin art which is done by molding and pouring a running fluid called epoxy. This fluid can be mixed with colored pigments to form beautiful abstract patterns and shapes resembling the mandala art form. Once the resin is dried, a fantastic glass-like finished product is ready. It's an excellent technique for people who prefer to avoid going for intricate art forms or traditional realism art. Abstract mandala resin art can be a wonderful therapeutic experience for all. However, it's a little expensive process, yet a nourishing art form for the soul and spirit.

Yarn Mandalas

Another ancient meditative technique of creating mandalas is the Yarn Mandala, called the Ojo de Dios or 'God's Eye.' The Mandala connects the spiritual world with the mind and body in a geometrical cosmic pattern. The Huichol(Indians from central Mexico) firmly believed that crafting an object was the easiest way to be one with cosmic energy. The Huichol people generally wove a pupil of black-colored yarn or a mirrored disk into God's eye seeking his protection. It is a unique mandala creation that has traveled across ages. The design begins at the center of the sticks symbolizing our inner center connected with the outer world.

Digital Mandalas

In the current scenario, people keep hovering in their vicious circle of life—aspirations, expectations, desires, lifestyle, work-life balance, survival, growth, and decline. Every aspect of life has become a massive task, and emotions are getting suppressed. Today, numerous creative forms of therapies and interventions have evolved to live a well-balanced and sane life. Mandala is one of the most result-oriented art therapy.

Technology has revamped and assisted in easing the complexities of the process. Now mandalas are ready in absolutely no time with the help of all the tools available on apps and dedicated mandala websites. The 'Undo' option on digital platforms is one of the most cherished advantages of the modern era, compared to when done traditionally. The process of coloring and creating new patterns is accelerated.

Though the emotional journey of self-finding one travel and experiences while working with a Mandala on paper is far more satisfactory than working with a mouse, the benefits gained from the process of being in it are no less. The perfection of the little imperfections of traditional Mandala making can't be wholly offset with the precision one derives through digital mandala making.

People who find working on digital mandalas fruitful can work on some undermentioned platforms. Only some of these platforms are free of cost, while others are available as in-house purchases.

Amaziograph: is a mandala app, widely available on all the platforms like Andriod, iOs, etc., easy and fun to use with exciting tools and in-built features.

Mandala Maker: is an app that can function only on selective platforms, iOS and iPadOS. It's a free app and worth a try.

Spiro: is a free mandala-making Android app that helps create seamless patterns while drawing a unique creation.

Mirrorgraph 2: is Mandala Android App with various brush and color options while creating patterns.

Others Apps that can aid in making digital mandalas

Mandoo

Mandala Maker: Symmetry doodle

Mandala Drawing Studio

Draw Mandalas

iOrnament

MandalaKit

Mandala Art Drawing & Colorful Mandala Creators

Mandala Maker 360

Doodle Master-Glow Art

Spirality

Mandala Me

MandalaGaba

Mandala Universe

Mandala Coloring Apps

Colorish

Coloring Pages

Mandalas Coloring Pages

Color Your World: Mandala

Radial

Chapter – 14

LANGUAGE OF SYMBOLS THAT MANDALA SPEAKS

Mandala is not just about creating random patterns. Every line, curve, design, shape, and color we put in a Mandala doesn't have a specific definition, but yes, it has relevance in totality, as a whole. Various symbols might appear while making an individual's Universe, but the interpretation is for signs currently present in the individual's psyche in that moment of creation. For instance, red has different meanings. It represents aggression, anger, and frustration but, at the same time, also depicts love, romance, and bonding. During the process, an individual's emotional flow decides the relevance of a particular color, shape, symbol, or pattern. If a person is in deep distress and has the same emotional outburst during the process, red may hint towards anger or rage.

Apart from the regular generic interpretation, an individual's interests, likings, and inclinations also play a significant role in making choices. His pedagogical understanding, spiritual predispositions, emotional quotient, and other aspects of one's life like psychological traits, cultural upbringing, value system, beliefs, experience, and interpretations also play a vital role in his formation and the result.

An individual's personality reflected in a mandala is sometimes a clear mirror reflection of his being in that moment or, at times, a complete dodge, too, if it's not done honestly or is pretense or prejudice.

A general overview of the meanings is mentioned further in this book, which may or may not apply in analyzing a mandala. Much information can be accumulated and evaluated based on an individual journaling process which should be true to this realistic depiction of emotions in that present moment of creativity and reflection. As per Carl Jung's interpretations and his 'Red Book' revelations, mandalas which are more abstract and made intuitively, have more honest and insightful disclosures. True self-expressions are visible while following an instinctual process unaffected by biases and pre-defined notions.

An Overview of Symbols: Shapes

Dot: the starting point of existence. The symbol of the self. It has no beginning, no end; it's eternal. The un-manifested unconscious self represents one's individuality. For details, refer to the explanation for the "Efficacy of a Dot" mentioned in the book.

Circle: one of the most widespread symbols used in Mandala Making. It represents wholeness and completeness. It is a symbol that depicts unity and integrity. A sign that is used primarily for expressing circular energies is Sun, Full Moon—often used in performing occult art.

Circle gives a sacred and safe space for emotions to grow and reveal themselves in the most accurate form. A combination of Dots within a circle also represents male energy, while a process without a dot exhibits female Power. The Union of both is the initiation of life.

Lines: Line is the basic, the first shape that a toddler draws without intervention from an external source or stimulus. The line can be horizontal or vertical. The former is a divider of two realms up and down. Sky and Earth, while the latter connects two energies, can be a divider between right and left.

Triangle: A symbol frequently visible in various art forms, including Mandala. If the vertex of the triangle points upwards, the energies, too, seem to rise in the direction of the spiritual zone. It also represents male energy represented by the element of fire. Symbolizes action and animation. However, if the vertex of the triangle points downwards, the powers seem to point towards an earthly, worldly zone designating creativity and sometimes the quest for knowledge. The downward vertex in a triangle represents female energy represented by the symbol of water. A union of all three vertices in an equilateral triangle depicts the Holy Trinity or the unification of Body, Mind, and Soul.

Star: a religious symbol representing cosmic order. It symbolizes the amalgamation of the self, the world, and the Universe. When related explicitly to the Mandala horizon, the star may tell independence, solitude, strength, sparkle, and stand-alone spirit. A star is a combination of two triangles, one grouting upwards while the other pointing downwards. When combined, the Union of fire and water has the Power to transform any metal into Gold.

Square: is the representation of our very existence in the world of materialism. It generally gets placed within the concentric circles in a Mandala. The square's four sides represent virtues: True self, Happiness, Eternity, and Purity. Four cardinal directions and four changing seasons signify movement and change. The lines and points in a square depict rationality and defined confinement to a space or borders.

Pentagon: represents the desire for perfection. A mandala's pentagon within a circular boundary signifies life and its influences or connections. I represent the number five or a five-pointed star that instills harmony and balance. It means all the five elements of nature are in perfect order within a human microcosm. The symbol aspires for coordination between our five senses for perfect functioning and absorption.

Heptagon: inclines towards a spiritual path. A seven-edged star draws the positivity of the number seven. It drives off evil and creates positive space for growth.

Hexagon: is the symbol of material aspirations infused with spiritual awakenings. A six-edged star, also called the "Star of David," is a combination of two triangles overlapping. The symbol resembles a honeycomb or the world of God. It's a storehouse of number six that symbolizes divinity, wisdom, love, and compassion.

Octagon: harmonizes and balances the soul. It's a shape that symbolizes rebirth, regeneration, infinity, transition, and resurrection. It is the advent of positive openings and fresh starts. Sacred architecture standing on octagonal structures has a divine connection and predispositions.

Rectangle: shapes in Mandala are used but could be more prominent. Generally, they don't dominate the space. Rectangles symbolize the four corners of the element earth, signifying strength and firmness. It's a safe place to build connections, things, and emotions and grow with them.

Arrow: The symbol of the Arrow depicts directions and targets. This symbol may help us to walk the inner search for our unique path. The Arrow, the sign of a war weapon, can also reflect the internal conflict and discord that needs immediate attention and required course of action to culminate.

Heart: The universal symbol of love that reflects care, concern, empathy, relationship, happiness, joy, the storehouse of treasures, values, and unconditional love.

Knot: The mystical or divine knot symbolizes good fortune, attachment, and indulgence. This symbol has a profound significance. It reflects some entangled emotions waiting to be released or loosened ends that need to be tied together. An inner introspection can help better understand the consistent surfacing of the knot symbol.

Cross: A cross symbol is prevalent in almost all cultures and traditions. The cross symbol with four extended arms represents four directions, seasons, noble paths, and virtues. The intersection of vertical and horizontal lines also represents the unification of males and females. The most prominent shape seen in cathedrals, churches, the symbol may appear in varied forms such as:

The figure of Christ or the crucifix

Ankh or entwined cross

T-cross, also referred to as Tau cross

X and Y cross

Swastika

Drop: A drop shape is one of the most commonly used shapes in a mandala. It can be a teardrop, dewdrop, or pearl drop, depending on the outburst of emotions at the moment of that particular mandala creation.

Spiral: has two ends. Positive and harmful, construction and destruction, life and death, and nature's dynamic. Waves are often visible in a whirlwind or a Maze. It represents fluctuations, deviations, or being in a pattern. On the positive side, a spiral also reflects psychic evolution. A clockwise movement aims toward the unconscious, wanting to manifest and liberate itself, while an anticlockwise direction urges it to move back to its core or inwards to the unconscious self.

Other Common Symbols and Their Significance

Animals

Very often, we may find in our mandalas the urge to color or create a particular shape or form that has some striking resemblance to an animal figure. This representation may connect with the traits, behavior, and characteristics of that animative symbol in the core of our existence. Millions and billions of species exist on the planet. Few, some, or many may have little or significant connection with our being. For instance, if I like to paint or have an intense indulgence in creating a lion-like symmetry in my Mandala, it may reflect my personality traits surfacing in that moment of creation. Being fearless, energetic, and roaring may be the emotions one is experiencing within the flow of thoughts in the conscious and subconscious self. Similarly, all animals have their distinct traits, habitat, characteristics, significance in myriad cultures, representation of Gods and Goddesses, magical powers, etc. the presence of these figures in an intuitive, abstract, symmetrical, or purposely designed Mandala may or may not reflect any connect or attachments to the same.

I find painting birds and butterflies soothing and resonating with my inner self. Birds as a symbol may represent characteristics such as freedom, flight, thoughts, creativity, horizon, wisdom, and spread. Conversely, butterflies may refer to beauty, symmetry, rebirth, transformation, etc. It all depends on what kind of emotions I am experiencing to establish a strong or weak connection with the symbols defined in any mandala.

A mandala may represent many things to an individual, but deep down the core, it reflects and represents order. It is understood, interpreted, and analyzed as a holistic self-created image of that unique directive one has been able to generate.

Wheel and Eight Spokes

The Dharma Chakra, or the Wheel of Dharma, represents a perfect universe. The Eight Spokes represent the Eightfold Path of Buddhism directed by Shakyamuni Buddha. The Middle Way or the Eightfold Path leads us towards liberation and renascence. The Eightfold Path consists of the Right action, Right View, Right Word, Right thought, Right Livelihood, Right Effort, Right mindfulness, and Right Concentration. The three elements of a wheel, hub, spoke, and rim symbolize the three main aspects of Buddhist teachings Wisdom, Courage, and Compassion.

The wheel with Thousand Spokes that resembles the radiance of the Sun represents the thousand actions and teachings of the Buddha.

Wheel with Four Spokes: represents the Four Virtues or the Four Noble Paths; True Self, Purity, Eternity, and Happiness. It also symbolizes four directions that the Buddha traveled and discovered the truth of birth, sickness, old age, and death.

Wheel with 31 spokes: represents 31 realms of existence in the ancient Buddhist Cosmogony.

Yin Yang

Mandalas closely connect with the symbol of Yin and Yang. These are the black and white half circles that swirl and twirl with one another., incorporating a dot of the opposite color present in both the forms, Yin and Yang—the visible presence of both the states in each other. Yin represents Earth, female energy, dark and passive, instinctual, irrational, and soft, while Yang is the male energy considered the source of light and wisdom. It adorns positive traits of being rational, sturdy, and firm. The symbol in Taoism (Chinese Philosophy) aims to create harmony between polarities.

Swastika

The Symbol of the Sun, Energy, Force, and Movement of the Universal Realm. The symbol of Swastika has been carried forward since ancient times and is widely used in modern times too. Spread across many religions and cultures; this symbol brings prosperity and abundant good fortune. In Sanskrit, "Swastika' means "conducive to well-being."

Particularly in Hinduism, the clockwise-facing direction (卐) is the Swastika, symbolizing the God of the Sun. At the same time, the anticlockwise order is the (卍), representation of the night or tantric activities of Goddess Kali called Sauwastika.

In the Native American culture, in the Navajo, Swastika represents a whirling log used for healing.

In Japanese culture, Swastika is a sign of peace and good fortune.

Sun

The Symbol of the Sun is a coming widely used pattern in mandalas. It's a symbol that represents the entire Universe. Energy and life are the emit-tent of this symbol. Vitality, energy, creativity, passion, and radiance are traits of the sign that we manifest in an individual through the Mandala.

The symbol of the Sun is present in ancient monumental structures, caves, paintings, etc.; this symbol has deep ceremonial and religious significance. Sun Gods and Goddesses are still the symbols of worship across religions, which symbolize the character of Power, light, and life.

Focusing on the center during meditation with the rays or waves pointing outwards can work on physical healing and spiritual growth. It manifests one's higher self.

Moon

The Moon symbol is also attached to the worship of Goddesses such as Luna and Isis. The triple Goddess, named Hecate, represents the phases of the Moon. Waxing, Full, and New Moon represent three stages in a woman's life Virgin, Mother, and wise old lady. Moon is a highly intuitive symbol. The crescent Moon or Chandra symbolizes timelessness, the impermanence of life, and resurrection.

The Hamsa (Evil Eye)

This Hamsa evil eye symbol brings good luck and prevents negative energies. It's a worldwide symbol of great fortune, wealth, good health, and productivity.

OM/AUM/OHM

In Mandalas, the sacred symbol of Om encompasses the entire Universe, energy, and mindfulness. The character of ultimate reality connects a soul with the divine powers of the Universe. The unification of the body, soul, and mind is the essence of this commanding symbol. The symbol embraces the amalgamation of the three powers of Hindu religious beliefs, and the three powers are Trimurti Brahma (The Creator), Vishnu (The Upholder), and Shiva (The Transformer). The symbol represents knowledge, strength, Self Awareness, Time (Past, Present, and Future), and Consciousness.

Elements of Nature

The elements of nature make the world work in order. Earth, Water, Fire, Air, and Space are five known elements that work in the human body to ensure the smooth functioning of the inner and outer Universe. A little disharmony among these elements could lead to chaos, disturbance, and ailments within the human body and the external cosmos.

These five elements are called Panchatattva – 'pancha' meaning five and 'tattva' meaning elements.

In a human body, these five elements appear as Earth and water present below the navel; fire is in the middle of the torso; air and space reside in the upper body.

In a Mandala, the water element is represented within a white circle or blue-green triangle pointing downward. It possesses a calm, serene, tranquil life state with female passive energy.

Air represents a blue triangle pointing upwards or a dot in the center representing male energy and value.

Ether or space represents a circle divided into six triangles uniting at the center point. Its purity, mobility, and etheric form give it an all-embracing motherly aura.

Fire represents a red half-circle, a red triangle, or rays or flames pointing upwards. It's the symbol of the Sun filled with energy, radiance, and warmth, as well as rage, anger, and destruction. It represents male active energy.

The Earth or Mother Earth symbol represents a cross inside a circle, a yellow square, or a brown, black triangle pointing downwards. It possesses female energies and values.

Floral Mandalas

Flower Mandalas are an instant urge and choice of many people as a chosen subject for mandala making.

Floral concepts in mandalas come in varied shapes and sizes. Having a sacred geometry, the symbol of the flower represents 'life,' compassion, and embrace.

For instance, the white rose represents love and spiritual awakening. Pink Dahlia symbolizes 'self-love.' The blue morning splendor spreads calm and contentment. Yellow Daffodil symbolizes hope. The lotus flower symbolizes enlightenment. Flowers represent various facets of life's attributes, manifesting in a mandala universe for positivity and self-growth.

Celtic Knot

A Celtic Knot comprises a series of overlapping or interwoven knots that don't have a clear start or end. Its enduring spirit is visible both in secular and religious forms. It symbolizes interconnectedness and continuity till eternity.

The Celtic knot symbol signifies the three forces of water, fire, and Earth, symbolizing unity and inclusion. There can be different representations of Celtic knots in mandalas manifesting good fortune and prosperity.

Celtic cross,

Trinity knot,

The Celtic love knot,

Spiral knot,

Dara knot,

Celtic shield knot,

Solomon's knot,

Celtic sailor's knot

The Chakras

Mandalas and Chakras have a long history of interconnectedness. Chakras originated in India and are complex entities within the human body. Chakra meaning a "wheel," refers to the energy points in a human body maintaining a balance between our emotional and physical well-being.

Chakras emit energy that facilitates the working of Human organs, mind, and intellect to the best of their potential. The Chakra Mandala represents seven concentric circular floral patterns radiating from the core to the outer layer running along the spine. Each of these even chakras has a name, number, and designated area of the spine from the sacrum to the crown of the head and health focus. Each Chakra has a color that symbolizes the colors of a rainbow or the color pattern of VIBGYOR.

The Root Chakra: lies at the base of the spine, in the tailbone area. It represents itself with the color 'Red' and evokes physical identity and stability. When this Chakra is aligned, one feels physically and emotionally secure and grounded.

The Sacral Chakra: lies below the belly button. It represents itself by the color 'orange' and evokes traits of sexuality and creativity. When this Chakra is aligned, one has strong self-worth.

The Solar Plexus Chakra: lies in the upper abdomen at the stomach area. It represents itself by the color 'Yellow' and evokes self-esteem and confidence. When this Chakra is aligned, one recognizes and manifests his unlimited potential and Power.

The Heart Chakra: lies right at the center of the chest, just above the heart. It represents itself by the color 'Green' and evokes feelings of love and compassion. When this Chakra is aligned, one manifests a sense of security, love, acceptance, and belongingness.

The Throat Chakra: lies at the throat. It represents itself by the color 'Blue' and initiates communication. When this Chakra is aligned, one can express freely. One would speak and listen compassionately and evoke confidence while expressing oneself.

The Third Eye Chakra lies between the eyes and forehead, also known as the 'brow chakra.' It represents itself by the color 'Purple' and is inclined towards intuition and imagination. Individuals can follow intuitive powers and see the far-sighted vision of actions and related reactions when this is in proper alignment.

The Crown Chakra: lies at the top of the head. It represents itself by the color 'Violet or White' and represents awareness and intellect. This Chakra connects to all the organs, including the brain and the nervous system. When the Chakra is aligned, all the other chakra work in tandem. Enlightenment, spirituality, mission, and purpose of life are defined in this Chakra to give meaning to life and its existence.

As these chakras are representations of human emotions and feelings, Any blockage or constraint in the flow of emotions in any of the Chakra can be controlled through understanding the art of Mandala by reflecting inside your soul and inner being.

Labyrinth

Commonly seen as a maze, we all have somewhere or the other has played a labyrinth to reach our goal, target, or final destination. In mandalas specifically, a symbol that resembles a maze is the lookout for the center of our life, our core. The sign directs us to unveil the hidden path where we genuinely find our life's mission or the reason for our existence.

Fish

Fish, or the water element, is the Christian symbol for Jesus Christ. Pisces's zodiac sign symbolizes sexuality, fertility, and productivity, having both male and female organs. The character generally presented in a pair depicts Union, relationship, love, abundance, and good fortune. A fish symbol placed in the north corner of the house brings prosperity and opportunities.

Bells: is the storehouse of evoking wisdom. Liberation and openness are symbolic of a bell.

Lotus: Symbol is a holy, sacred symbol in Buddhism and Hinduism. The Petal symmetry of the flower symbolizes harmony and balance. It is the only flower that blooms and bears seed simultaneously, thus representing the law of cause and effect.

Essence of Colors

Colors have always attracted me since my childhood. I could barely answer when someone asked me about my favorite color. I loved all. Even black, which had something different to gauge my interest and eye. Little was I aware of the meaning of this colorful world. I remember, in India, we celebrated Holi (Festival of Colors). I was interested in something other than enjoying the festival. Instead, the only thing that implored me to hold my constant gaze on was a platter full of different colors. As if I just wanted to immerse myself in all the shades possible. This exact feeling remains alive in me to date. The colors have a profound language. Unspoken and unsaid, they reveal much about one's personality, aura, vision, and character. I could quench my thirst, this colorful hunger, only when I entered the world of Mandalas. The sacred space where I could play and experiment with all the shades of colors. So many aspects of invisible beings that get an opportunity to play their part and dance in harmony with the perfect acoustic melody of diverse colors. It's not without an unfathomable reason that we get attracted to a few colors and show acute resentment towards some. My little understanding of this world, just my viewpoint based on the scholarly research done by eminent personalities in this area, can help the seeking minds.

Colors evoke different feelings in different entities. Understanding what emotions and sentiments emerge when we get attracted toward a specific color or shade is essential. Colors profoundly impact our chakras and our state of mind or psyche. They rejuvenate us and, at the same time, also reveal the melancholy of the heart, soul, and mind. If we choose a particular color, we must reflect our emotions while drawing ourselves to it. Colors can instill enjoyment, curiosity, and cheerfulness into a negative mindset. It's essential to find you connect with the right color palette. Color therapy can positively influence human emotions and feelings toward a desired path or trail. This technique is widely tried and tested in the Chinese, Egyptian, and Greek cultures and is prevalent in many other prophecies.

We all know the fact that colors emerge from white light. When the rainbow colors are rotated or spun together, white is the universal color visible to us. The Chakras, or the healing source, are deeply rooted in different colors evoking a distinct trait at every level of consciousness.

There is a total of seven groups represented by the seven colors of a rainbow. Red, Yellow, and Blue belong to the family of primary colors. These primary colors, when mixed, create the secondary ones.

Yellow + Blue = Green

Red + Yellow = Orange

Red + Blue = Violet

Red+Yellow+Blue+Green+Orange+Violet = Indigo

Let's study what each color brings out in us. All the colors have a dual aspect. Individuality is not just Black or White. Individuality reflects multiple elements; some are active momentarily, while others may be dormant. Few may be present but resisting to surface. Mandala helps to curb the resistance, ignite the positive static traits and dwindle the active negative color synergies.

Red: Red is the most prominent color of the palette. It is a color of love and passion, emotional fire and energy. It has a spiritual zone as it's the color of the first Chakra, meaning it's rooted in the self-consciousness of the body. But on the contrary, it's also the color of rage, anger, lust, and aggression. It represents the Color of the blood, the Planet Mars, the Gods of War, and likewise. A strong inclination towards this color and dominance of the same in our art can hint towards a robust mindset and a strong urge for transformation.

Yellow: is the color of energy, Power, and Vibrancy radiating from the core or the center. It's the color of the Sun God spreading positive vibes, cheerfulness, happiness, and umph. It's the color of the third Chakra symbolizing enlightenment, wisdom, emotions, and freedom. It propels solid intuitive powers. But on the contrary, a not-so-vibrant shade of yellow, a pale or a dirty yellow represents sickness.

Blue: the color of the sky above and the color of deep oceans and seas. It was spreading serenity, tranquility, calmness, flow, and protection. It represents more of a female energy. It's the color of the fifth Chakra, the throat chakra. Oratory skills, creative vision, and self-awakening are strengths of the color blue. The dominance of this color in the art can represent psychic independence and solid intuitive emotions. The negative aspect of the color symbolizes introverted nature, self-centeredness, and withdrawal.

Orange: is a storehouse of abundant energy, joy, and vibrancy. It's the color of the sunrise and sunset. Orange color Evokes energy, enthusiasm, new beginnings, optimism, and radiance. Positivity and self-confidence rule this color zone. It's the color of the second Chakra, symbolizing sexuality and relationships. The other side of the orange represents dusk. It was the setting down of energies at one point, leading to the rise of future possibilities and opportunities.

Green: is the color of prosperity, growth, nature, and peace. It represents the balance of nature. It has a naturally soothing, relaxing, and healing effect on our beings. The color of the fourth Chakra is strong filled with abundant love and compassion. On the flip side, green evokes a strong feeling of jealousy, suspicion, and wariness.

Indigo: it's deeper than the Blue. It's the color of the Spiritual Self, mystical and meditative by nature. The color of the sixth Chakra, to the forehead chakra, represents our sixth sense, or the third eye. Incredibly instinctual can hover around both the positive and the negative emotions in a moment.

Violet/Purple: is a color obtained from red and Blue. Violet is the color of the seventh Chakra, also known as the crown chakra. Spiritual by nature, the violet color evokes cosmic energy enlightened state of mind. On the other hand, this color points out the need for self-introspection or reflection within oneself.

Pink: is also a product of a combination of white and red. Hence, it follows the traits of both. On the one hand, the color represents compassion, love, and passion but also a desire for peace, protection, and contentment. The more one increases the content of white, the lesser the rage and obsession.

White: is the color of purity, unity, peace, and calmness. It's the color of the seventh Chakra. Hence spiritual calling is visible. When all the colors are spined together, what one gets is white, which symbolizes the absence of everything. White is open and accepting. It neutralizes either side. Which also means that it fades away vigor and energy. It's the symbol of a dove that takes a plight of freedom, camaraderie, and unity. The most ecstatic and blissful color among all. It's also the color of new beginnings and endings.

Black: the most mysterious of all colors, Symbolizes darkness and death. It is the color of the night. All the secretive and hidden truths lie in the shadow of paint back. That's why we refer to it as 'Black Magic.' It evokes feelings of suppression, depression, anxiety, suffering, and mourning. But simultaneously, it brightens all shades of life when they contrast with black. The true joy of life, the dawn, is only seen after the darkness. Hence it catalyzes growth and evolution. Black color in Mandalas inclines towards a self waiting to be explored and accepted. It is the color of transformation. The color is also associated with might and power. Many of the Gods and Goddesses in Indian Mythology and other religions have also embraced black to reveal their strength and supremacy.

Grey: has several shades. It can spread warmth but at the same time can be cold too. Vitality and lethargy both go hand in hand. The color of nature represents wisdom, aging, and experience. Essentially, it's the color of ash, mist, and cloudy sky, which also means a lack of clarity and insecurity. We often refer color grey as a transitory phase where one is trying to move from an unconscious being to a conscious, enlightened state of mind.

Brown: is a mixture of red and green. Abundantly present in nature with a touch of motherly love. It's the color of the Earth, mountains, wood, the roots, all pointing toward strength, survivor, feeder, protector, and nourisher. The color also represents autumn, the fall—period of sustaining oneself with the harsh winds and unseen challenges. If used as a dominant color in a creative space, the color might point to a crowded area and energy that needs liberation and acceptance.

Gold: is radiant. Its shine is impermeable. It's the color of one of the most precious metals that increase its worth and value. Gold color used in a Mandala uplifts the energy and vibrations. It can create its glitter no matter what space or combination it is in. The Sun is called the "Golden Sun' which emits light, energy, cheerfulness, and growth. It's precious and highlights the path of spirituality, higher state, and realms of life, such as realization and Buddhahood.

Silver: is cold. It neutralizes the heat of Gold into calmness and serenity. Contrary to Gold, Silver is the color of the Moon's celestial bodies. Its gentle temperament creates a radical harmony and balance amongst varied elements in an entity in a given moment.

Rainbow

A unison of seven colors forms a bridge. This symbol is the connection between the Universe and paradise. The Goddess of the Rainbow is Iris. Based on the rainbow concept, Mandala refers to wholeness, inclusiveness, transformation, and inner healing. The seven of a rainbow also resonate with the seven layers of the chakras in a human body, unveiling the seven layers of consciousness. Crossing the rainbow bridge means being one with eternity.

Meaning of Numbers Reflected in a Mandala

Numbers have always had a unique existence and deep-rooted significance in our reality since ancient times. In the sixteenth century B.C., Pythagoras proclaimed that numbers were not just restricted to mathematics but had a divine presence in the spiritual world.

As per Pythagoras, "Number is the ruler of forms and ideas and the cause of gods and daemons." Then came numerology, which gave cosmic importance to numbers. Every number had a meaning. Carl Jung, in his extensive research, linked numbers with synchronicity. He said, "a meaningful coincidence of two or more events where something other than the probability of chance is involved." Numbers come to the surface due to changes happening in our unconscious realm.

When you have the exact numbers repeating repeatedly, they mean something profound. They are trying to tell us things that demand our attention. It's a spiritual awakening seeking its way out through the language of numbers. Numbers hold different meanings across varied cultures, but a standard derivation and deduction that fits in most cultures and religions and applies to mandalas also exist here. Carefully look out for the language of your soul spirit trying to communicate or guide you through. The numbers appear instinctively during the creation of an individual's Universe. As your soul is conscious in the process, so does the numbers. It is essential to discover one's unique meaning in those numbers.

So the crux is finding your meaning rather than jumping to easy conclusions.

Number **0**: has no value when alone but adds worth and buy when it stands against the other. Zero represents the womb or the point of origin. It is the number that stores one's potential. It seems to be nothing, yet it is everything. Symbolic of wholeness, completeness, divinity, and purity

The synchronicity of numbers is not generic. They are personal and hold secretive meanings depending on the thoughts and emotions one carries during the mandala process. The traditional definition of numbers is essential rather than explaining or deriving meaning from those numbers.

While journaling, one must take account of what one feels at that moment when any number appears. No matter how vague the idea may seem, anything random that strikes the conscious level becomes a part of the journaling process. What kind of triggering does one find while scanning through the number? The feeling of awe, excitement, restlessness, joy, curiosity, fear. Any emotion that flashes by may have a meaning, so put it on.

Zero symbolizes an empty circular boundary, a perfect space for creating your distinct Universe.

Number 1: Number one stands tall, Ponting upwards. The number represents immense strength, Power, agility, precision, and self-empowerment. It's the number of the originator, decision maker, and male energy of Yang. Unlike the feminine nature of the number zero, which is more giving and enduring, number one is selfish and revolves around the self.

Number 2: as the number reveals, it operates from a duality mode. Two sides of a coin, light and dark, true and false, yin and Yang, up and down, black and white, in and out. Two bonding together or two splitting apart. It may point toward harmony and balance or towards a rift or a conflict.

Number 3: number of the trinity, thought beholds Power and wisdom but is generally misunderstood as unlucky and unfortunate. Mind, Body, and Soul; Life, Birth, and Death; Past, Present, and Future; Father, Mother, and Child, Number 3 is an instinctual number and brings good fortune. Three times lucky, a hat trick, three cheers. Self-development and creativity are born from this holy sphere. Egyptian culture, Christianity, Celtic mythology, and Wicca are all positively associated with the number 3.

Number 4. Four is all about positive, soothing vibes. Four seasons, phases of the Moon, Four noble Truths, Four cardinal directions, four corners, and four elements of nature are all symbolic of being entirely in the present time. Number four represents direction, logic, analysis, the balance of nature, movement, and divine awakening.

Number 5: number five is a calm, composed, sensual number. It represents an addition to a fifth element in the category of Ether or space. The Five senses symbolize adaptability, new beginnings, and changes. Because this number links to play, it may call for freedom, adventure, and exploration. It's the number that brings choices.

Number 6: number six directly hints towards our sixth sense. Hence the Power to know above the rest. A connection between the earthly and the spiritual World. In a Mandala, if you find the number six, it may also evoke feelings of compassion, love, care, spiritual peace, inner peace, health, creativity, and joy.

Number 7: mysterious seven is the vastness, depth, reach, expanse, and spirituality. Good fortune and synchronicity are grounded in this number. Seven musical notes, Seven oceans, seven vows, seven rebirths, seven days of the week, seven chakras, and seven rainbow colors symbolize our life's journey. It's a number that calls for deep introspection as it entails hidden treasures and can exist within a soul spirit.

Number 8: number 8 is the bridge between the conscious and the unconscious self. Number eight represents wisdom, togetherness, and pacifier. It's a valid number that co-relates with the theory of cause and effect. Positive actions bring positive results, while negative actions bring suffering and pain. Number eight Is the number of Karma, birth, and storehouse of good and evil. It represents eternity, infinity, and reincarnation. It points out strength, courage, infinite potential, action, determination, and wit.

Number 9: is the number that is associated with the higher consciousness or the high life state. The state of realization and learning depicts through number nine. Related to life's mission and unique purpose in life, number 9 represents wisdom and enlightenment. It's a sacred number that revolves around positive energy, creativity, compassion, endurance, perseverance, and contentment. It's a number of the ninth level of consciousness that we generally refer to in our spiritual connection.

Number **10:** is the end of the cycle of numbers. Being a combination of one and zero, it represents both the male and female Power, their Union. Ten is a number from where a significant change is born, which may lead to positive beginnings, new opportunities, new directions, and transformation of thought and actions. Keeping oneself aware of the changes happening around that are trying to reveal something imperative will lead to the opening of spatial blocks and unsolicited constraints.

Number **11:** it's a number more often recurring in different forms, at other times, in different ways as your spiritual messenger is trying to converse with you and make you understand something related to the changes happening in your life at that moment. It varies from person to person and their unique circumstances. 'The eleventh hour' is generally referred to as situations that demand immediate attention. Change may be positive or negative but requires instant acknowledgment followed by deeply introspected action. Being highly intuitive, this number eleven might function through impromptu visions such as dreams, flashes, or incidents. Born with all the key strengths of number one, the traits of number eleven multiply manifolds.

Number **12:** is a unique combination of one and two, referring to the harmony, order, and balance of the cosmic World. It's a creative number that holds firm expressions of self and the Environment. Twelve months in a year, twelve Greek Gods, twelve zodiac symbols, and twelve kinds of personality prototypes. Twelve represents the inner voice of the soul.

Number **13:** thirteen is one of the scariest numbers. The deadliest and most unfortunate number in the number system is thirteen. It represents darkness, death, mourning, ill health, bad luck, and other negative pre-conceived notions with the number thirteen. 'Friday the 13th' is called Doom's Day in prevalent cultures and traditions. But on the contrary, this number is a sign of liberation and transformation. This number is the number of Karma or thoughts, deeds, and actions. It's an angelic God's number healing the pain and suffering. Thirteen moon cycles in a year represent changes, renewals, and the fortune of a lifetime.

Chapter – 15

MANDALA AND THE TEN WORLDS

I never knew that my connection with my spiritual World almost two decades back would drive me through the most satisfying, joyful, and insightful journey of my life. Everybody is born with a unique, distinct mission for his life that only they can fulfill. This mission is not only to quench an individual's thirst for desires, wants, and aspirations that lead to his happiness but to embrace others in his Environment through open arms, compassion, and empathy and spread happiness. There is a greater purpose in life. The mission can be anything; someone may be an artist or a singer, an educator or a performer, an activist or a leader. The idea is to awaken oneself to the true purpose of their life. This enlightenment can lead to realizing one's dreams passionately but also add value and joy for others.

Some may realize their dreams early in life because of the sheer clarity and focus they maintain consistently, while few may have to change the trajectory of their life to understand their ultimate purpose. Life has its ways of teaching us the fundamental law of existence, which is spreading happiness.

I encountered the philosophy of Buddhism 22 years back. Spiritual enlightenment gave me the strength and courage to understand the course of life and the meaning of hardships we assail in our life journey. Remaining unperturbed by the trials and tribulations of daily life, I perceived the concept of "Ten Worlds "through my faith. I could meticulously see the realm of Ten Worlds through my Mandala and never less thought of incorporating it in my book as well. I hope this concept helps you connect with your conscious and subconscious self to understand your emotions and feelings better.

Self and Emotions

Mandala is a world of bringing out our emotions on a surface through random or structured patterns, symbols, shapes, etc. Sometimes we deliberately or unintentionally tend to hold back these emotions within ourselves. These emotions accumulate within and are trapped inside. The negativity or the urge to free oneself from the weight of such trapped heavy feelings later becomes serious ailments, mental disorders, behavioral issues, and other unpleasant outcomes.

One needs to understand and accept emotions, whether positive or negative. These result from a specific action or perception in a single moment of life. The moment that passes through and leads into another moment and then another to the final moment of life or even beyond it to eternity is never constant. Hence no emotion stays forever.

The feelings or emotions classify into ten words. Hell, Hunger, Anger, Animality, Rapture, Tranquility, Learning, Realization, Boddhisattva, and Buddhahood (Buddhas)

It is not untrue to say that every single day, morning till night, moment to moment, our state of life oscillates between highs and lows. Quite possibly, We may wake up feeling joyful, satisfied, and full of enthusiasm towards the start of the day. Moments later, an unanticipated occurrence or uncontrollable action in our Environment can put us into a state of Anger or rage. Hence, we shift gears in our ten worlds in a moment's flash.

An excellent tasty breakfast can bring a smile and a world of tranquility into action. Heavy traffic can bring out the World of hell just in an instant. After which, a good piece of music brings us back to a temporary state of rapture Only to ignite our Anger and rage on a broken car and its owner who unintentionally caused us suffering. Little later, we reach our destination to find that though being late, things are still under control, and the World hasn't turned upside down. It makes us less wary, and we enter the higher World of thinking and validating our overreaction to the situation, entering into a world of realization and suddenly changing our subtle emotions into hungry spirits of fame and appreciation as soon as we find our boss praising our junior for his commendable work on a shared project.

In the above instance, do you notice how fast we change one emotion to another? One low state of life into a higher state and vice Versa. Energy is oscillating amongst different worlds in a particular given moment.

Classification of Ten Worlds

Buddhism classified this visibly infinite range of the various states of life into ten inner "worlds." This unique concept of the "Ten Worlds" can bring about a deeper understanding of the changing nature of positive and negative tendencies that work in our life due to our fundamental character or nature. Of these ten worlds, the most influential World that is inherent in all energies is the World of 'Buddhahood.' We all are Buddhas. It means that an individual possesses all the Ten Worlds.

Mandala making and these ten worlds go together. While creating our universe, we should let these worlds flow freely without putting any boundaries or confinement on them. We may move from World to World or emotion to emotion in less than a fraction. Sometimes Anger, sometimes contentment. The play of emotions is to be without any biases during our mandala creation. Mandala-making is a soulful process; that's why every emotion comes from deep within our core. The present 'moment' of our life comes alive through the Mandala. All the reflections we've had from hell to Buddhahood represent the variations in that very moment. As we assume The creation to be completely intuitive, whatever thoughts flow, they have a deep connection with the color, pattern and shape we tend to choose. Sometimes the images we create are distinct and sharp, while mandalas may be abstract at other times. Structured or asymmetrical, all are meaningful. Moreover, our emotions find a path to get heard, which brings inner calm and peace to all the turbulences one carries deep inside.

The depth of this concept is co-related with mandala art. When we talk about ten worlds, one should know that every active World also contains the other nine within that moment. If I am in a world of Anger, the other nine worlds are also present at that moment. The World of 'anger' becomes dominant, and the other nine are latent.

Mandala helps move from the first six lesser worlds to the four higher ones. Even though one may be suffering or going through a rough patch and experiencing the World of Hell or Animality, there is the possibility of transforming this situation into a positive and sharing the World of Hell or Animality. There is all the possibility to change this situation into a positive life state and move into the higher worlds.

Let us know a little more about each World, helping us to reflect those in our immediate Environment.

The World of Hell

This World is the lowest state of life where an individual seems completely helpless. Rage is the best term to define this state of suffering where living itself becomes painful. We look at this World with a vision of agony and hopelessness.

The World of Hunger

We have numerous desires and wants that we want to accomplish in life at a jet's speed. In this World, we suffer due to our cravings in life that seem to be insatiable. Hungry spirits hover in the World of Greed so much that aspirations become desperate.

The World of Animality

Thoughtless, impulsive reactions govern the World of Animality. It's the World of animal life where selfishness is at its peak. Individuals lose the sense of right and wrong, good and bad. The law of the jungle becomes prevalent where the weak are threatened and suppressed by the strong. The rationality behind actions goes for a toss. Individuals here design their sufferings and lead to future self-destruction.

The World of Asuras

They are demons present within our five feet, body including Demons of Egoism, self-centeredness, superiority complex, inferiority complex, and arrogance. This World carries a false image of oneself, putting a double-faced idea of the external Environment. Pretend, prejudice, jealousy, resentment, self-depiction, and hypocrisy drive the World of Asuras.

Hell, Hunger, Animality, and the World of Asuras form the four evil paths.

The World of Humanity

From the four evil paths, we move towards a better World, The World of Ordinary human beings. The World of humanity represents a life state that is calm and composed. Nichiren Daishonin writes," The wise may be called humans, but the thoughtless are no more than animals. "Here individuals have a state of mind to differentiate between the right and the wrong. To be rational in action, one needs to put a constant effort into exercising self-control. Even kind and generous humans can touch a low vulnerable life state, falling into the evil trap or devil's play. Hence, they need constant guarded over evil thoughts and actions.

World of Heaven or Tranquility

The World of heavenly beings enjoys a life state of Joy and Happiness. When we fulfill all our intuitive, social, spiritual, intellectual, or worldly desires, we eventually experience bliss. As the proverb says," Nothing lasts forever." This World also can't last for a lifetime. As soon as the joy turns into a challenge, the World of Heaven tumbles down instantly, inflicting suffering and misery back into the life state.

Mandalas are a perfect medium to vent out all the above six states of emotions that we generally operate or function from, mostly in our day-to-day life. With the help of the Mandala art, we can transcend from the lower six worlds to the higher four noble worlds of Learning, Realization, Seeking Spirit, and, ultimately, The Self Awakened state of life.

The World of Learning

In this colorful World of Mandala, we cross our self-imposed boundaries and accept that we need to open our path to absorb and imbibe the impermanent nature of life. Both joy and suffering together are perceived as life. It's a world where we begin to find happiness in our struggles and obstacles in daily life. There is no life without hardships. However, the nature of our battles may differ, but there is no life without challenges. The moment we learn and imbibe this element, we move from the lower life state to a step further toward the higher self.

The World of Realization

The World of realization is one of the ten higher Worlds of self-introspection. A state of life where we can rationally look deep inside our reactions and actions to the external Environment. A world where we take charge and complete responsibility for our actions and control over our Environment. Emotions in this life state are above our earthly attachments and instinctive desires. A conscious effort to feel our feelings and work upon ourselves can elevate our low-life state into a higher one.

The World of Seeking Spirit

In Nichiren Daishonin Buddhism, this World is called the World of Boddhisattva. It means that an individual still walking the path of learning and realization is not yet wholly a Buddha. This emotion is expansive where I rise above the notion of "Me, Myself, and I" to 'US' and 'WE'.

A world where we are compassionate towards others' sufferings and sorrows too. Nichiren Daishonin writes,

"Even a heartless villain loves his wife and children. He too has a portion of the Boddhisattva world in him". Hence our emotions in this World are ruled by compassion and empathy.

The World of Enlightenment

As most of us know, The World of Buddha is the World where we enjoy being alive. Unsurpassed wisdom, love for humanity, and kindness epitomize this tenth World. The Supreme World is inherent in everyone and can manifest through a conscious self.

Mandala-making helps us to explore these worlds through colors, shapes, and forms. Our choices represent our dominating worlds and perceptions. Our refine thoughts can help us become a better version of ourselves.

These ten worlds containing the other nine worlds themselves become 100. Hundred get multiplied by the ten factors (appearance, nature, entity, power, influence, internal cause, relation, latent effect, manifest effect and their consistency from beginning to end) becoming a thousand. Multiply the 1000 realms by three realms of past, present, and future, which sum up to three thousand realms in a single moment of life. This concept helps us to understand the immense potential within an individual. A moment in one's life, three thousand possibilities of existence. Thus the change in the mindset of the life condition of a single individual can bring an immediate change in his Environment, which ripples down to our community and society. An individual can influence other people around him. My negativity can be transferred to others, while my positivity can encourage others. For this simple reason, we get influenced by others' states of mind too. The connection we have with other people determines their life state as well. For instance, if a person likes to criticize or complain frequently and dwells in a lower world will also be attracted to the same company of others who believe in pulling people down. Still, if one dwells in a higher world longer than usual, compassion and kindness will likely be the critical parameters for choosing one's company.

The ten worlds come into the form of ten life conditions that almost each of us experiences at some point. The first six worlds are visible instantly in our life and cnvironment as soon as a triggering situation or circumstance occurs. At the same time, the remaining four worlds come alive only when we consciously seek and aspire to be in these worlds in our everyday life despite the presence of unanticipated unpleasant experiences. The World of Buddhahood comes slowly but surely. Still, it requires an intense effort and constant work to learn, realize and accept our tendencies, transform them, and direct them towards positivity, productivity, and self-development.

It's precisely what a mandala can bring into one's life—overcoming negative tendencies, switching to higher worlds quickly, and transforming one's core values and mindset to cherish the best possible outcomes visible in our external Environment.

The unique aspect of the concept is that in these nine worlds, there is always an aspect present to balance the negative emotions. This positive aspect is that the tenth World of Buddhahood entails absolute happiness unaffected by any of those nine worlds or external stimuli. It is a condition of pure joy. A mandala helps us experience this absolute joy even amidst our life's challenges and sufferings—a point where being alive is the greatest joy.

The moment we begin with the mandala-making process, we enter the higher life states of learning, realization, a bodhisattva (cause and effect), and Buddhahood.

In the course of a passing moment, we may experience different worlds as a response to the stimulus generated in our immediate Environment. Here is the situation, we all operate from one dominant World where our activities are centered. I may work from a world of Anger, hell, humanity, etc. This World will help me analyze my Mandala or the unique universe one creates at that moment operating from a dominant world. The fluctuations in the World may happen depending upon the flow of our thoughts and emotions. Engaging in a mandala creation uplifts our low-life tendency into a higher one and eventually sustains more in the highest World of Buddhahood.

Being in the highest life state does not mean we will never experience the other nine from that moment onwards. But on the hand, we learn to accept that these states are a part of life. By experiencing pain, suffering, hell, and Anger, we can know and feel the worth of joy in our lives. "To cherish every spring of our life, we must undergo the harshness of a winter." Mandala takes us through all these turning and reflective points where we can calmly introspect and reflect upon our actions and turn the bitterness or overwhelming emotions into a springboard for growth, self-awakening, and development.

Our negative instincts and immediate Environment will not control us, but we can build a harmonious entity and balance between self and Environment.

This mandala creation process can help us tap inside to know the following:

1. What exactly resides in my heart at that very moment?

2. What is my life condition?

3. Which World do I operate from? (if I am consistent with my mandala activity, I can get an honest answer. I can determine which worlds I

mainly oscillate in. I come to understand exactly which areas do I need to work upon).

This process helps us take complete responsibility for our situation and accept that no matter how grave the life circumstances may be, we can change them for the better. Complaining erases good fortune, while gratitude builds the storehouse of treasures. The Mandala process is a way to open our path of being grateful to life and the people revolving around it. Even those who bring out the worst in us are to be thankful because they help us realize the hidden negative emotions that make us suffer. Once we stop getting negatively affected, these emotions turn into an insightful journey.

The process reveals the relationship between our life conditions regarding the inter-connected World and the Environment surrounding us. It empowers us to bring a required change in our ongoing life.

Chapter – 17

MY JOURNEY WITH MANDALAS

Mandalas are a soulful process for me. Just like a surrender to the divine, when I create my universe, I completely surrender myself to the creation and the emerging thoughts.

I want to share my mandala journey experiences with you. The thought I come across and the process I follow. It's less of mandala analysis but more of the holistic flow of emotions and the urge to create a unique art whenever I sit with a concept.

I love to work with intricacy. Detailing brings a lot of calm and peace to my mind and soul. My mandalas take anywhere between 80-100 hours to completion of it. The ones I do are intuitive but symmetrical. They are all conceptual by nature, and I let the title be absorbed fully by my mind and soul before initiating the process.

Music and fragrance are the key factors that help me to keep my focus intact for long hours. Any music works for me. But yes, I have analyzed that peppy, energetic, and vibrant music reflects bold, striking patterns, while slow, sinking music reflects subtleness in my strokes and composition. You will find it for yourself once I remember and explain a few art pieces I created in the past.

I start my art by preparing my base for painting. I love working on wood. As a nature-loving person, choosing wooden surface for most of my artwork makes me joyful. However, I have tried working on paper, canvas, terracotta, glass plates, etc., with a lot of textural play. Every base had a completely different output and thought involved. One should use all kinds of surfaces and paint materials to feel the difference and distinctness of the divine process.

Also, mistakes happen during the process. It's natural. But when I feel that too many recurring mistakes restrict the flow of my emotions, I prefer taking a break. It's good to carry on for a moment, fighting your resistance, but if the mind gets overpowered and the heart is overwhelmed, pausing is advisable as it will add to the anxiety. One should switch to physically releasing such negative powerful emotions to evoke balance and harmony. Taking a walk or a jog, cycling, exercising, or playing a sport is suitable for releasing energy.

Never rush to complete the process; instead, absorb and reflect on the emotions that want you to tell you a lot about the inner turmoil and seek answers to questions arising from the soul.

I choose colors randomly before starting anything new, and if I feel the need, I add to the selected panel. As I love colors and a lot of colors basically, my creations have more than 10-15 color variations. As a beginner, it's good to choose your palette intuitively and keep it concise, with a maximum of 3-5 colors.

I draw my structures randomly, circles and their measurements are done entirely at the spur of the moment. Yes, I do draw a minimum order of symmetry. Sixteen sections to start, and if I need to increase the total order, I do it during the process. I choose my subject, but I don't choose the pattern. I let the design take its due course during the process. It helps me to analyze and reflect upon the emotions I go through deep within and seek answers to the chaotic mind that never stops thinking instead of overthinking.

Let me take you through a few subjects I have worked on.

Let's recollect what Mandala means.

Mandala is a Sanskrit term meaning a 'circle,' just like a life meant to take a full circle for its completion. Mandala centered around a dot representing an individual born with a unique mission and purpose in life. A dot has no definitive beginning or end because it's eternal, just like life that flows freely, transiting from one human form to another.

Mandala 1:

Title: Elements of Nature

Medium: Acrylic on Wood

Subject details:

The intricately done Mandala art represents the five elements of nature present in our human body Water, Earth, Fire, Air, and Space. Each part has a distinct role in maintaining harmony in the human body structure. Even if one goes haywire, we experience discomfort at varied levels.

72% water, 12% Earth, 6% Air, 4% Fire, and the rest Space exists in our body. However, the interrelatedness and existence of one in all the other elements simultaneously is a beautiful concept to delve deeper into.

Colors and patterns help us evoke these elements deep in our minds and soul, bringing the spiritual self alive.

Shades of blue represent water, green represents earth, yellow/red exhibits fire, grey tones picture air, and metallic shades represent space, creating a symphony that calms a restless mind and parks a galloping heart.

Spiritualistic, meditative, and illusionary, the Mandala represents all elements within a human form.

Flow of emotions

There was a sudden urge to draw something representing the five elements of nature. I started with a dot that represents the beginning of my universe. Water occupies the Mandala's most significant areas, spreading calmness, flow, and composure. The strokes turned into representations resembling fish motifs. These were not thought of earlier and emerged as an impromptu symbol. Fish represents life, an abundance of good fortune, and fertility. Fish symbolizes swimming through life's challenges dauntingly. I could relate to these emotions and have a deep connection with them. Most of the strokes in the Mandala are pointing upwards. Considering my life state in that moment of creation, these upward-pointing strokes inclined towards the opening of self and expressions. The division of elements landed appropriately by their required proportions. In totality, the Mandala brought a sense of harmony and contentment. The radiance emitting outwards enhances positivity and empathy. The balance of colors in this particular creation also points towards the balance of elements in the self environment.

Mandala 2:

Eight Fold paths

Medium: Acrylic on Wood

Subject details:

The intricately done Mandala art depicts divinity, enlightenment, and an authentic way of life. The right direction leads to the right action. A deluded mind is an ordinary being, while an awakened one is a Buddha. Buddha resonates with calmness and peace; his teachings are called the Eight-Fold Path.

The Earthy Colors and patterns in this Mandala help us to evoke these elements deep in our minds and soul, bringing out the spiritual self alive. The carefully thought design represents each of the Eight paths unveiled by Buddha to lead humanity in a harmonious direction.

Right Speech

Right Action

Right Mindfulness

Right Effort

Right Understanding

Right Thought

Right Livelihood

Right Concentration

Spiritualistic and meditative, the Mandala represents the divine yet an ordinary soul who propagated peace and harmony.

Flow of emotions

I have a connection with the spiritual World for more than two decades. The teachings of Buddhism have a profound impact on my being. I realized that world peace starts with one individual ready to change their inner self to bring out that change in the external Environment. I resonate with the teachings. Taking responsibility for the situation and changing oneself inside out will change the World around us. This thought was the reason for the conception of the Mandala "Buddha and his Eightfold Path." I wanted to bring the element of Buddha life. Thus I painted the buddhas face separately to drive attention to the central point featuring his perceived divine facial expressions. The correct path gets constructed around the center of the wheel.

After the formation of the wheel at the center of the Mandala, the pattern and symbols generated intuitively to bring out my inner thoughts on the subject of divinity and human revolution in one individual. The symmetry order is purely based on considering the eight paths Buddha taught. Most of the mandalas are golden, symbolizing radiance and enlightenment. The inner feelings of tranquility came through effortlessly in this artistic creation, but it took much perseverance to continue. Almost 100 hours went into this awe-struck creation. The Mandala is therapeutic as it helps me hold my concentration and attention span for a long time. Looking at the Mandala, I can control my anxiety and commotion and stabilize my irrational thoughts into a well-directed and controlled flow.

Mandala 3

Title: Winter Turns to Spring

Medium: Acrylic on Wood

The intricately done Mandala art represents that every harsh winter of our life in terms of obstacles, sufferings, challenges, etc., is short-lived. There is Nothing that stays forever. Every sorrow has to turn into joy, and after every joy comes challenges. Hence absolute happiness is undeterred by life's good or bad. The only thing constant is change. The Mandala depicts the impermanence of life.

Here in the Mandala, every winter color changes into its vibrant spring tone. It symbolizes that every winter of life turns to spring, but never has it reverted to autumn. There are more than 18 shades in this Mandala. The combinations came from instinct, which, in the end, ended up in perfect harmony and balance every color tone of winter turns into a brighter tone of vibrant spring shade depicting that every winter has to turn into spring..

The Mandala is meditative, spiritualistic, and thought-provoking. It Brings in a lot of positivity and hope.

Flow of emotions

The Mandala came into existence when there was a rough patch in my life, but I had the ichinen to surmount all hardships and fulfill my dreams. I am naturally attracted to working with many colors, so this Mandala and subject gelled perfectly together. White paint has highlighted the presence of all the other colors, propagating and spreading peaceful vibes. The upward strokes reflect confidence and courage in thoughts and actions. The floral motif that emerges in the end, shows a blooming phase of life, embracing joyfully the trials and tribulations that come as a part of the journey. The use of varied colors and tones reflects various facets and emotions that parallel each other. Whether it is Anger and love, compassion and withdrawal, prosperity and lull, all exist together in a moment..

Mandala 4

Title: Flora and Fauna

Medium: Acrylic on Wood

The intricately done Mandala art represents the oneness of man and his Environment. No one can exist or grow in isolation. We all are a part of nature that embraces both Fauna and Flora. Being aware of our existence and mission on this planet and protecting our Environment, not only for ourselves but the generations to come, should be a conscious effort made by each individual.

The colors and patterns in this Mandala are a constant reminder of such spiritual awakening to our mission. Our 'being' working in tandem with nature's creations and mutual co-existence will make this world a better place to be true.

Spiritualistic, meditative, and illusionary, the Mandala represents being one with our Environment.

Flow of emotions

I am a nature-loving person, and flora and fauna have been the central concept of many of my artworks; however, they are the first of their kind in my mandala representation. The pattern in the Mandala had no preconceived notion. It came completely instinctual. The colors of the Mandala were an inner urge of the moment. After that, the structure got created layer after layer. Distinct shapes, star, floral, and fish motifs are visible in this creation. One common aspect among all these symbols is growth, abundance, and bloom. The instinctual combination of colors, blue and yellow, green and blue, reflects balance and neutrality. The symmetry brings harmony and calmness to the soul.

Mandala 5

Title: Fish Takes to Water

Medium: Acrylic on Wood

The intricately done Mandala art represents the relationship between fish and its habitat, water. The Mandala projects a pair of fishes bringing in the sexuality traits of both male and female energies. This mandala creation is unique, distinct, and eye-catching.

The color combinations are different and striking and generate a natural attraction towards it. The shapes are uncommon yet perfectly complement each other to create balance, stability, and poise. The colors and patterns in this Mandala are a constant reminder of such a spiritual awakening to our mission. Our 'being' working in tandem with nature's creations and mutual co-existence will make this world a better place to be true.

Highly enticing and appealing in concept and color combinations. The Mandala creates a beautiful symmetry, both rotational and reflective. Spiritualistic, meditative, and illusionary, the Mandala represents being one with our Environment.

Flow of emotions

This Mandala creation was different. It was not to be made as an intuitive mandala, as my concept was quite clear. I wanted to create a circular harmony of fish in a certain way. The outline of the Mandala and its structure was quite clear inside. But the twist happened when I started working on this creation. My palette that I initially thought of and the actual outcome is two extreme entities. The concept, though, remains the same. As a symbol, fish is welcome to an abundance of good fortune and good health in life. I incorporated the sign of fish in the Mandala. Still, unexpectedly, the fish turned out to be in pair and not single, which was the original plan of action that had yet to materialize.

Moreover, this was my first Mandala, where I created the center after completing the outer and inner layers. This creation with a lot so surprises and insightful learning for me. The fish symbol in pair refers to unison, bonding, and compatibility. It was a phase where I could visualize the connection and the bonding with my better half. Understanding and respect are the key ingredients to build a strong relationship. I could see all these facets turning strong in my personal life. There may have been an inner impulse to bring those emotions out at that particular moment which came as a pleasant surprise to me. The true magic of Mandala making is where the hidden feelings find their unique path to flow.

Mandala 6

Title: Light of The Sun and the Moon

Medium: Acrylic on Wood

Are all mandalas symmetric? No. Mandala, when done intuitively, is a reflection of the inner state of life. If it is undertaken purely as a reflective art, it's not necessary that creates visual symmetry, but yes, it does create mindful balance. This very Mandala is an asymmetric representation of the light of the Sun and the Moon. I was able to freeze The subject but not the structure.

The thought behind this Mandala was to bring in the concept of existence. The Sunsets every day to give way to the light of the moon. So without the radiance of the Sun, there can be no gentle touch of the moonlight. The Sun and the Moon hold an impeccable bond that gives a purpose to their existence. The Sun rises in the East to spread its light, but that docent means the moon disappears. It's just waiting for the Sun to move under the horizon.

When the Sun meets the moon, an eclipse forms. The Sun symbolizes our ego, and the moon governs our emotional being. After introspection, I could relate to my urge to pick up this subject. There was an emotional conflict where I oscillated between my ego and my higher emotional self. My restlessness and disharmony were quite apparent during the process. The number of mistakes I made in this entire creation was by far the highest made errors ever in my mandala creation. The chaos was visible. But in the end, no matter how dark our World may seem, the light overpowers the night. The discharge of emotions through a Mandala gets clarity of thoughts, harmony, and self-balance.

Mandala 7

Title: The Rainbow of My Life

Medium: Acrylic on Wood

Flow of Emotions: A tribute to my Late Sister Meenakshi Chauhan!

My first intuitive Mandala creation is a tribute to the most lovable, trustworthy, guiding star of my life, who now bless all my actions from the above heavens. My late sister, a true warrior for me, passed away two years back, fighting cancer. She was one person who loved me unconditionally and supported me in all my actions, guiding me in my difficult times and giving me abundant hope and courage to fight for my right. I wanted to grow as an artist, and she gave me wings to fly. Her trust in my dream was my strength. I wanted to create something unique for her. Before realizing what art I wanted to pursue, my lifeline took a form of the brightest twinkling star from the heavens above.

I wanted to create something that reflected her personality, contagious positivity, and Spirit. The only thought that stroked me was to create "A Rainbow Mandala. " My sister, Meenakshi, had traits of all the rainbow colors in her. Her colorful features included her passion for educating children, compassion for the needy, unconditional love and support for her family, a hope-filled attitude, courage, a charismatic leader, and a gem of a person. She was a lioness, never took injustice, and fought truthfully.

I wanted to create an art that illuminated her Spirit. This Mandala is an ode to the 'Rainbow of my Life. 'To capture her Spirit and manifest it through my art. Every stroke, pattern, and color reflects my love, longing, and void for the person I most cherished. No words or expressions are enough to pen down the deluge of emotions I underwent making this art for my beloved sister. Love her till eternity, until we meet next.

Chapter – 18

INFERENCE

Mandala art connects a body to its soul and a soul to its body, where the mind is the liaison between the two. "Life at each moment encompasses the body, mind, self, and environment. " The book's contents are meticulously worked upon, considering the emotions one may encounter in a single moment. It is essential to give the needed space and time for the feelings to find their unique path. Emotions must be clear and free-flowing, followed by a suitable call to action.

People who find it difficult to express themselves in words and are not comfortable trying traditional or modern art forms must once try to be consistent with the mandala art form for at least 30 days to see a significant change in their thought process and their ability to deal with situations occurring in daily life differently and many times positively.

Most of the book's insight comes from the author's real-life journey. It's tried and tested. When we go to the doctor for a cure for a specific disease or ailment, we trust him completely. We consume the prescribed medicines without acquiring formal knowledge about them to feel good and healthy. Similarly, mandala art can be transformed into healing art only when we trust the process and consistently apply the guidelines stated in the book.

Some of us may not engage with mandala spiritual art for a long time. It is acceptable because each of us has a unique calling which may or may not be Mandala Art. Our spiritual awakening may rest in some other art form or specialization that brings immense peace and happiness for us and everyone in our Environment. But to know where our happiness lies, it's always advisable to try things. Everything remains wishful thinking only when we gain experience by doing it ourselves.

Mandala art is not a modern concept, but it's a practice followed for ages in varied cultures and religious realms to find the core values of one's being. It's a deep introspection within that helps us to be one with ourselves. Inner peace, happiness, and contentment are the prerequisites for a happy external environment. Just 10-15 minutes of daily mandala-making and journaling can drastically change our temperament and perception. Self-acceptance is complex and, once done, opens impossible ways for self-growth and development.

My life and its encounter with Mandala art can bring positive change or calm your World of chaos and disruption.

I am sending loads of good wishes for you and your family's well-being. May you create a universe filled with abundant happiness, good health, and good fortune.

ACKNOWLEDGMENT

I am expressing my deepest gratitude to the following individuals, whose unwavering support and encouragement have been invaluable in creating this book.

First and foremost, I extend my heartfelt appreciation to my mentor Dr. Daisaku Ikeda for being my pillar of strength. Your life journey has propelled me to take actions that were once a dream. I am truly indebted to you for life and eternity, my mentor in my heart; I walk the path of my desires and passion, adding value to my life and many more lives.

I am grateful to my teacher, Arijit Bhattacharya. Your guidance, expertise, and belief in my abilities have been instrumental in shaping my writing journey. You have taught me the importance of perseverance and pushed me to exceed my limits. Thank you for your relentless dedication to my growth as an artist.

I extend deep gratitude to my mother, Smt. Kawal Suri, thank you for always being there. Your constant encouragement, patience, and belief in my dreams have inspired me. I am grateful for your support and the countless sacrifices you made to ensure I had the opportunity to pursue my passion.

I want to mention my Late father, Shri Ved Prakash Suri, and my sister Late Smt. Meenakshi Chauhan who are no longer with us, yet their memory and impact on my life remain ever-present. I wish they could be here to witness this accomplishment.

My most profound appreciation goes to my loving husband, Vikas Bhatia. Your unconditional support, patience, and understanding have been immeasurable. Thank you for creating a nurturing environment that allowed me to immerse myself in my passion and for your endless encouragement. Your love and belief in me have been my greatest strength, and I am eternally grateful for your presence in my life.

To my wonderful children, Eishti and Awadh, you have brought joy, laughter, and inspiration. Thank you for understanding the countless hours I dedicated to my passion, cheering me on, and reminding me to take breaks. Your love and support have been the driving force behind my determination to complete this milestone.

I extend my gratitude to my dear brother, Dr. Pradeep Suri, for always being there to provide encouragement and support. Your belief in my abilities and constant motivation has kept me focused and motivated throughout this journey.

To everyone mentioned above and to those whose names may not appear on these pages, please know that your contribution to this book, whether big or small, has made a significant impact. I am forever grateful for your unwavering support, love, and belief in me.

Thank you all from the bottom of my heart.

Sincerely,

Dr. Shipra Bhatia

BIBLIOGRAPHY

Adams, Lily. The Mandala Garden: Cultivating Inner Harmony and Wholeness.

Baker, Samuel. Mandalas: A Path to Self-Realization and Spiritual Awakening.

Collins, Daniel. The Mandala Oracle: Awakening Divine Guidance and Wisdom.

Cooper, J.C. An Illustrated Encyclopedia of Traditional Symbols. London: Thames and Hudson, 1979

Fincher, Susanne F. Creating Mandalas for Insight, Healing and Self-Expression. New York

Johnson, Sarah. Mandalas: A Journey into the Self.

Jung, C. G. (1960). Mandala and the Quest for Wholeness: A Journey of Self-Discovery.

Jung, C. G. (1964). Mandala and Self: The Path to Wholeness.

Jung, C. G. (1966). The Symbolic Life: Mandala as a Gateway to the Unconscious.

Jung, C. G. (1972). Mandala in Art Therapy: Unlocking the Creative Unconscious.

Jung, C. G. (1973). Man and His Symbols: Mandala as a Universal Archetype.

Jung, C. G. (1976). Mandala and Active Imagination: Navigating the Inner World.

Jung, C. G. (1977). Mandala: The Integration of the Self.

Jung, C. G. Dreams and Individuation. In collected works, Vol. 5. Translated by R.F.C. Hull. Princeton, NJ: Princeton University Press 1985.

Lewis, Victoria. Mandalas: A Journey to the Soul's Inner Landscape.

Mitchell, Robert. Mandalas: A Gateway to the Divine Within.

Phillips, Melissa. The Healing Power of Mandalas: Restoring Balance and Harmony.

Reed, Samuel. Mandala Magic: Tapping into the Inner Wisdom of Sacred Circles.

Robinson, Jennifer. Sacred Circles: Exploring the Spiritual Significance of Mandalas.

Huyser Anneke. Mandala Workbook: For Inner Self Development.

Smith, John. The Art of Mandala: Exploring Sacred Geometry and Symbolism.

Thompson, Michael. Mandalas: Unlocking the Mysteries of the Universe.

Turner, Benjamin. Mandalas: A Visual Journey to the Depths of Self.

Turner, Grace. The Mandala Oracle: Awakening Your Inner Wisdom and Intuition.

Wilson, Olivia. The Art of Mandala Meditation: A Path to Inner Peace and Self-Discovery.

Mandala: Sacred Symmetry, Better than Pi, https://betterthanpi.com/mandalas-sacred-symmetry/

The Ten Worlds; Chapter 2, Sokaglobal.org, https://www.sokaglobal.org/resources/study-materials/buddhist-study/the-basics-of-nichiren-buddhism-for-the-new-era-of-worldwide-kosen-rufu/chapter-2.html

7 Chakra Jewlery – Kustoms by La'Sha, LLC. https://kbl4me.com/products/earrings-7-chakra

Wisdom from the five elements of nature || Pancha tattva. https://www.cycle.in/Happiness-Wellbeing-Wisdom-From-The-Five-Elements-of-Nature

Aunt Lydia's Mandala Doily – Craft For The World. https://craftfortheworld.com/aunt-lydias-mandala-doily/

Unlock the Power of Color: Your Brand's Secret Weapon | SpellBrand®. https://www.spellbrand.com/branding-color-strategies

Healing Tools – A y n i A l c h e m y. http://aynialchemy.com/techniques-tips-and-healing-tools/

numbers Archives - Showit Blog. https://ipekwilliamsoncoaching.com/tag/numbers/

| Ichinen Sanzen Pt4UK Mahayana Buddhism. http://www.buddhastate.com/2012/05/ichinen-sanzen-pt4/

Two words to ban from all your arguments - David Hare. https://davidhare.com/2013/01/29/two-words-to-ban-from-all-your-arguments/

Scan the QR code now for a captivating mandala experience with 2 hours of free live session – Your journey to inner peace begins now!

Feel free to email if unable to access the QR CODE

liveyourcore2023@gmail.com